CW01044226

THE
FENDER
AMP
BOOK

JOHN MORRISH

THE FENDER AMP BOOK
A full descriptive history of Fender's
classic instrument amplifiers
by John Morrish

A BALAFON BOOK

First British edition 1995

Published in the UK by Balafon Books, an imprint of Outline Press Ltd,
115J Cleveland Street, London W1P 5PN, England.

ISBN 1-87-154794-6

A catalogue record for this book is available from the British Library

Printed in Hong Kong

Art Director: Nigel Osborne
Design: Sally Stockwell
Editor: Tony Bacon

Typesetting by Type Technique, London
Print and origination by Regent Publishing Services

95 96 97 98 5 4 3 2 1

CONTENTS

Leo Fender was a remarkable man. He was no musician: indeed, contemporaries record that he was virtually tone deaf. Certainly he could never tune the guitars that bore his name. And yet, his instruments revolutionised the way music was made. Nor was he an engineer. He had no more than a working knowledge of electronics. But in the far-off days of vacuum tubes (or valves), that was enough to build the practical amplifiers that would give his instruments their voice.

Mostly, he was an intensely practical man: a tinkerer, an enthusiastic maker and mender of things, never seen without a screwdriver and a pair of pliers in his pocket. He coupled that with a strong entrepreneurial streak and a liking for the company of musicians. He knew how to find employees and collaborators whose skills would complement his own, and how to drive them nearly as hard as he drove himself. These things were to spread the Fender name across the world.

BORN IN A BARN   Clarence Leo Fender was born on August 10, 1909, in Anaheim, in the heart of Orange County, California, named after its principal agricultural industry. Fender's parents, Clarence (known as Monty) and Harriet, were orange growers themselves. Leo was born in the family's barn: the Fenders didn't build themselves a house for another year. An early photograph shows a stern-looking farmer in dungarees, his wife holding the baby, and behind them the barn, two horses and a couple of basic wagons: it could be Grant Wood's famous painting 'American Gothic'. Within 60 years their world would disappear beneath the concrete and asphalt of what is now a densely populated and industrial area of California.

Leo himself had no desire to live off the land. It was a time of new and exciting technological developments. He became fascinated by the emerging world of radio and electronics. At the age of 13, he built his first crystal radio sets, even before broadcasting had arrived in southern California: he would listen to ship-to-shore communications. Later he became a radio ham.

He also had musical interests, taking a couple of years of piano lessons in his teens and playing saxophone in a high school band. He also built an acoustic guitar at about this time, and, once amplifying tubes became commercially available, from 1928, combined both his interests by building and renting out primitive public address equipment for sports and social events.

FENDER RADIO STORE   After school and junior college, where he studied English, business, mathematics and law, he married Esther Klotzky in 1934 and then went north to work in the accounting department of the state highways division. Later he transferred to work for a tyre firm, but was made redundant when the business was sold. So he returned to his home county and his original interests and, at the end of 1938, opened the Fender Radio Store on South Spadra Boulevard (now Harbor Boulevard), Fullerton's main north-south thoroughfare.

Fender sold electrical appliances, records, musical instruments and sheet music as well as doing repairs and supplying public address systems. It was now that he came into contact with several people who were to prove significant in the Fender story. Don Randall was a fellow radio ham and electronics enthusiast some eight years younger than Leo. Before World War II, he had a radio parts business, and supplied the Fender Radio Store. Unlike Leo, who was excused military service because he had lost an eye in a childhood accident with a farm cart, Randall took his electronic expertise into the army. The two did not meet again until the war was over, when an association began which was to last 25 years.

DOC AT THE RADIO STORE A shorter-lived connection, though as significant in its way, was that with Clayton Orr Kauffman, known as Doc, a professional violinist and lap steel guitarist who had earned a reputation locally as a music teacher by performing in shop doorways and attracting both customers and prospective pupils. He arrived at Fender's shop one day just before the war with an amplifier for repair. The two had a discussion about electric pickups for lap-steel guitars, and this led to plans for a collaboration to design and build instruments and amplifiers. That would have to wait until the war was over.

There were no new radios for sale during the war, because the factories had turned to armament production, but the government ensured that there were spare parts, so repairers were kept busy. At the same time, local musicians would bring in their instruments and amplifiers for servicing, enabling Leo and his repair man Ray Massie to take a close look. Kauffman had already had some experience in working on electric steel guitars for Rickenbacker, which was also established locally, and the three men began to work at their own designs. The conditions were in place for a commercial breakthrough.

In the first place, the lap-steel (or Hawaiian) guitar, which had enjoyed phenomenal success almost as a novelty instrument during the 1930s, had become popular with the Western swing musicians of the day. The instrument sits horizontally on the player's lap and the strings are stopped by a bar which he slides up and down the neck with one hand while he picks with the other. A simple instrument with only a rudimentary soundbox, the steel guitar benefited greatly from the introduction of amplification. Other players and instrument makers were experimenting with attaching magnetic pickups to "normal" (then often called "Spanish") shape guitars.

Amplified sound had been around almost since the invention of the thermionic valve or vacuum tube by John Fleming in 1904. The triode, the first amplifying valve, was patented by the American electrical engineer Lee de Forrest in 1907 for use in the detection circuits of radio receivers, converting radio waves into barely audible sound to be picked up on headphones. His first audio amplifier, to make the sound louder, was patented in 1911. The circuits were quickly picked up and improved for use in radios, record playing equipment and the early sound cinemas: de Forrest had also invented the optical film sound-track by this stage. The patents on all early valve circuitry were held by the American Telephone & Telegraph company and Western Electric, but these companies permitted the valve manufacturer RCA to reproduce the designs in the handbooks issued to anyone buying the valves.

When Leo Fender and Ray Massie produced their first amplifiers they took them straight from these valve manuals, as did everyone else. No royalties were paid; nor, apparently, were they demanded. During the war, Leo had repaired and modified amplifiers and steel guitars: he and Kauffman applied for a patent on a guitar pickup in September 1944. Moving into small scale production seemed a natural step. A joint company was formed by Leo and Doc, to be called K & F (for Kauffman & Fender), funded in part by a design for a record changer that they had sold for $5,000.

At that time, steel guitar and amplifier were considered one item. The amplifiers and steel guitars K&F built, during 1945, were finished in a grey crackle paint. Surviving examples have two sockets and are seen with and without a volume control. Grilles were either in wire mesh or in a coloured cloth, sometimes with the distinctive K& F logo, featuring a lightning flash. Their power output was no more than 4W (four Watts). It is said that about 1,000 of these sets were built in the year or so that they were in production.

The K&F steel guitar (left) was, with its matching amplifier, Leo Fender's first commercial product.

K & F

Leo Fender's first amplifier, the K&F, was only available as part of a set with the steel guitar. Its tiny output, usually estimated at about 4W, destined it for students and beginners.

When Leo Fender and Doc Kauffman introduced the K&F amplifier, electronics was in its infancy, a matter of assembling a tiny number of stock components in accordance with their

The K&F products were built in a shed behind the Spadra Boulevard radio shop, by Leo and Doc working after shop hours and at weekends, sometimes until late at night. With the end of the war, civilian manufacturing was once again encouraged, and Leo was nursing plans for expansion. But Kauffman had had enough. "It costs a lot of money to get into large scale production," Leo told BAM magazine in 1980, "and the 1930s depression was still fresh in Kauffman's mind, so he didn't want to get involved. He had a ranch or farm in Oklahoma and he was afraid that if we got overextended on credit he might lose it. He thought he'd better pull out while he had a full skin, so in February of '46 he left it all to me."

PARTS & CABS By this time Don Randall had returned from his war service and was working for a man called Francis Hall as general manager of Radio & Television Equipment Company of Santa Ana, California, supplying local radio shops, including Fender's, with parts. From 1946, R&TEC took on

The badge of the K&F Manufacturing Corporation was more impressive than its factory, which was a shed behind Leo Fender's radio shop. The logo's central device, a treble clef with a lightning bolt through it, was later used on the first Fender products. This K&F amp (right) has a volume control in addition to the usual two jack sockets. No two amps from this period are exactly alike.

manufacturers' instructions. The grey crackle finish K&F amp was no exception. Its circuitry is based on the examples supplied by the valve manufacturers in their applications manuals. Its simple wooden cabinet and bent-metal chassis posed few problems for such small-scale manufacture. Nonetheless, it was obviously successful enough to encourage Leo Fender in his plans for large scale expansion. The whole Fender amp story began with this little wooden box.

distribution of the new Fender company's products. At the same time, Leo moved his manufacturing to new premises, two 30ft by 60ft corrugated iron huts on South Pomona Avenue. Not long afterwards, at the end of 1947, Fender sold his radio shop to another long-term associate, Dale Hyatt.

By now, the first amplifiers and guitars bearing the Fender name were being produced. Called the Model 26 by collectors today, they came in polished

wooden cabinets, complete with wooden handles, and had 8in, 10in or 15in speakers. Presumably because of the cost of true grille cloth, these had soft felt fronts, in red, blue or gold, but with chrome strips over that for protection. Most people insist that the 10in is the only true Model 26.

Don Randall and his colleagues had the task of trying to sell the amplifiers and steel guitars. "At that point, shortly after the war, competition was very limited," he says. "With proper promotion, and exercising the knowledge we had

Fender produced three types of amplifier in this cabinet design. This is a Model 26 Deluxe in maple. Oak and mahogany were also used.

MODEL 26

The first amplifier to appear under the Fender name. The Model 26 designation is usually applied to the 10in Deluxe.

Confusingly, the Model 26 control panel and nameplate is used on both the Deluxe, with a 10in speaker, and the Professional, with a 15in. There are many variants in both construction and appearance. The example above has horizontally mounted valves: others have the usual hanging-down valves. The Princeton (left), an 8in speaker student amplifier, looks similar but has no controls or control panel.

of the product, it was easy for us to go out and start doing business. We were probably one of the only companies in the business that had the technical

background to do the job. We knew what we were doing."

The 1947 catalogue lists three amplifier models, all in Model 26 style, the 8in Princeton, the 10in Deluxe and the 15in Professional. There was nothing particularly new about these amplifiers, but they did have the advantage of being well engineered and robust. Amplifiers were available from Magnatone, Epiphone, Gibson, Oahu and many more, but Fender's were designed to achieve reliability and serviceability on the road. For instance, logic would suggest that the place for the heavy glass valves was at the bottom of the cabinet. But experience taught Fender that musicians would use the open back

The control panel arrangement (above) of the Super (originally named the Dual Professional) became standard on later tweed models. The part of the chassis bearing the controls and input sockets appears in a recess cut out from the top rear of the cabinet.

SUPER

The Super began life as the Dual Professional, and was the first twin speaker amplifier. It used a pair of 6L6 tubes to produce an output of about 16W for use with steel guitars.

Leo Fender introduced the Dual Professional (later renamed the Super) in 1946/7 to capitalise on a sudden surplus of 10in speakers. He placed them on an angled baffle board in a heavy-duty lock-jointed cabinet and covered it with an early type of "tweed".

of the cabinet for storing spare leads, tools and so on, so he put his valves at the top, usually hanging down (though some Model 26s mount them horizontally).

One question mark was over the wooden cabinets, which, while looking magnificent in a new state, deteriorated very rapidly in use. They were jointed with internal angle-iron, which was not as secure as it might have been. The next generation of Fender amps, from about 1948, tried to tackle that with a new cabinet construction, with what are called finger-joints at each corner and a new covering of durable luggage linen.

Another long-serving Fender associate joined the company in February 1948. George Fullerton was not long out of school, and spent his time moving furniture, repairing radios and playing guitar with a local band. Leo invited him to work at the new Pomona factory, where he joined a workforce of no more than 15 people. He was to become factory foreman.

At this time the steel guitar market was still booming, thanks in part to the influence of the guitar studios, which sold a musical education door to door. "They'd go out and canvas the neighbourhood," explains Randall, "and they'd get a lot of students into these so-called studios that were teaching steel guitar and accordion. Some of these studios had as many as 3,000 students!"

STUDENT SETS Fender always kept in its range a student model guitar and amplifier: originally this was the wooden cabinet Princeton ($45.50) and a matching guitar ($36.50). Later, the Champion took on the role, paired with a guitar in what was called "mother o'pearl plastic": the set cost $98.50. The amplifier was named by Don Randall, who, as the man who had to sell the equipment, was usually given the task of coming up with suitable names: "I always tried to stay away from things like 'student' or 'beginner', because nobody wants to be a student or beginner."

But that was just the start of what was clearly a profitable business for all parties (dealers enjoyed 100 per cent mark-up on the guitars). "These kids were from middle class families, mainly, people who wanted their kids to have whatever they could afford for them. And they couldn't deny them a musical education. So schools'd sell them a series of lessons, and they'd have to have a guitar," says Randall.

Ever ready to oblige, the Fender company sold the schools simple Spanish type acoustic guitars which it packed six to a crate at $16.95 each. Later the students would move up to the basic steel type. "What they used was an open E tuning where you could put a bar across and move it up and down to play 'Nearer My God To Thee' and a few little things like that. And then the studio would say, 'You know, your child has exceptional talent. But it can't be exploited on this type of instrument....' This was a step-up sale, eventually winding up, when double-necks and triple-necks came out, in bigger, better and fancier guitars."

Naturally, Fender provided a full range. Its first double-neck steel came with the move to the new premises. But an interesting side-effect of this emphasis on the steel guitars was to slow the introduction of the solid electric Spanish-type guitar which Fender had been experimenting with for some time. Leo had built an experimental model without a proper body during the war years. In 1949, he was working on the first Esquires and Broadcasters, but Don

Randall for one was not sure he could sell them. He took a prototype to a trade show and was laughed at: "It was called everything from a canoe paddle to a snow shovel." As he explains, "The studios didn't think they could adequately teach a Spanish type guitar that you had to place your fingers in certain places to obtain the chords. They were used to teaching classes of 15 to 20 at a time with steel guitar, where they could say you put your bar here and move it to here. If you had a good ear you could move the steel and make it sound like something."

But Fender's electric Spanish was never aimed at that market. It was intended for the working musician who wanted to be heard above horns and drums. Leo and his associates took it directly to the musicians and marketed it themselves, initially. Only after it had established itself among that group, and particularly among the first players of rock'n'roll, later in the decade, did it have a mass-market appeal.

With the new guitar came new amplifiers. The expensive steel guitars had always been partnered with the Professional amplifier. It seems that a trend in the amplifier market towards 12in speakers meant that Leo could buy surplus 10in drivers at an advantageous price. He put these to good use in a new flagship model, the Dual Professional, featuring two speakers on an angled mounting board. Launched in 1946, it boasted a new covering of ribbed cloth, an early variant of the type later to be known as tweed. Renamed the Super, it was recommended to match the new solid guitar, renamed the Telecaster, when that was launched in 1951.

TV Front The remaining amplifiers in the range were remodelled, starting with the Professional, now renamed the Pro Amp and put in a new "TV-front" cabinet with a top mounted chassis with the controls facing upwards for new accessibility. This box takes its name from the televisions of the day, in which the screen would appear from a rectangular surround with rounded corners. In this case the screen's place was taken by the brown speaker cloth. The cabinet was wrapped in luggage linen, initially in a tight vertical weave in a white colour, covered with a lacquer that rapidly turned golden brown. From about 1950, this was changed to a variant of the familiar diagonally ribbed "tweed" linen that is still used today. The new linen promised to be much harder wearing than what had come before.

The Champion student amplifier, which began with an 8in speaker (the 800) in 1948 and went to a 6in version (the 600) in 1949, resisted the 'tweed' look until 1953. The 800 was covered in grey linen, the 600 in a cream and brown cloth with a plasticised "Naugahyde" finish which matches the early guitar cases. With its three-valve circuit, it represents the simplest of all amplifier designs, and yet its performance is such that it has long been a favourite with collectors and players, despite its tiny 3W output.

At the time, its normal, undistorted output would have been considered quite loud enough by the student players it was aimed at. Later, its appeal to players lay in the fact that it could be made to distort at comparatively low levels and then fed either to a PA or a larger amplifier. The fact that its most appealing quality was an accident of design rather than a feature is a paradox to which we will return.

Distortion in an amplifier is, fundamentally, the sound of circuitry in distress. In particular, it arises when one amplifying stage expects the next stage to produce more output than it is capable of supplying. When the Champ

CHAMPION 600

The most famous of all practice amps, the Champion or Champ stayed in production in various guises for more than 30 years.

The Champion 600's two-tone Naugahyde finish is unique among Fender amps. It was sold as part of a set for students with a matching steel guitar. Later, its willingness to distort at low levels made it a studio favourite.

This 600's control panel (right) omits the word "Champion": the use of the name seems to have been disputed. Fans of "Spinal Tap" will note that the volume control goes to 12.

was designed and marketed for use with the low powered guitar pickups of the day, the level of amplification provided by its single pre-amp valve was not

enough to "overdrive" its single power output valve. Later, with more powerful pickups, higher signal levels would pass through the pre-amp valve, demanding ever more amplification and volume from the power output valve.

Fortunately for lovers of the overdriven sound, it was quite incapable of supplying the output levels required, and the distortion was the result. To a greater or lesser extent, all of Fender's early amplifiers display the same characteristic, although as their power output increases the point at which the distortion sets in moves further back. Of course, by modern standards they were all tiny amplifiers, rarely putting out more than 15W, and then into speakers that were simply not capable of taking the power, another (though much less sustainable) source of distortion.

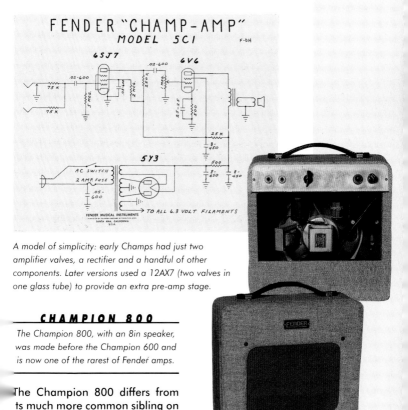

A model of simplicity: early Champs had just two amplifier valves, a rectifier and a handful of other components. Later versions used a 12AX7 (two valves in one glass tube) to provide an extra pre-amp stage.

CHAMPION 800

The Champion 800, with an 8in speaker, was made before the Champion 600 and is now one of the rarest of Fender amps.

The Champion 800 differs from its much more common sibling on account of its larger speaker, its early tweed covering and archaic engineering details, such as the way the output transformer is bolted to the loudspeaker frame. This was not a recipe for reliability.

With increased demand, and all the manufacturing works being carried out in the two existing sheds, it was time to build a new unit to house Leo's office and his research and development facilities. A new block-built structure was erected on the same site. For the first time washroom facilities were provided: previously staff had had to use those in the nearby railway depot.

The new electric guitar was taken up by Jimmy Bryant, best known for his work in a duo with pedal steel player Speedy West: the pair's television appearances provided priceless publicity and boosted sales. But Leo was not prepared to rest on his laurels. He had plans for a revolutionary instrument, the electric bass, and that needed amplification to match. The results were the 1951 Precision Bass and the first Bassman amplifier. Hedging his bets, Leo was careful to advertise the amp, as he had previously advertised the Pro Amp, as being suitable for string bass too. It used a 15in speaker in a TV-front cabinet with a closed back with two ports and employed two 6L6 output valves which supplied the maximum power available at that time. It was the beginning of a formidable amplifier line.

The power of advertising, early 1950s.

Leo liked to introduce something new every three months, whether a guitar or an amplifier. In 1952 a new amplifier, the Twin Amp, was introduced. With two 12in speakers, and an extra valve in the pre-amp section, this now became the top model in the range. It was intended to be a partner for the new luxury Stratocaster guitar, although because of problems with the latter's vibrato arm the guitar did not appear for some time. Fender had a policy of continuous improvement, inside and out, and the Twin would usually be the first to benefit from any changes. It also ushered in a new cabinet design, the "wide panel" tweed style, in which the grille cloth area is squared off and extended to the sides of the cabinet, leaving wide panels above and below. All models were brought into this uniform look.

By the end of 1952, it was becoming apparent that a further relocation would be necessary. The noisy and dirty processes involved in amplifier and guitar manufacture were no longer acceptable in the residential areas of Fullerton. So Leo Fender found a new site, on South Raymond Avenue in the east of the town, and plans were put in hand for a move.

This wide panel Deluxe has the control arrangement common to almost all Fender's tweed amps. The control panel is part of the amplifier chassis, made to appear in a cutaway at the top rear of the cabinet. The pointer knobs are stock items from electronic parts suppliers.

FENDER DELUXE

The tweed Deluxe is one of the most popular of the Fender amps with collectors and players alike.

The Deluxe was one of the first amplifiers Leo Fender produced in his own name. The wide panel tweed variant shown here was produced from 1952/3 to 1955/6. Early models (5B3, 5C3) use 6SC7 pre-amp valves. Later (some 5D3 models) they were replaced by the miniature 12AX7 valves still used today. The Deluxe is a low output amp, prone to distorting at comparatively low levels, which makes it excellent for recording or playing through a PA.

In a number of ways 1953 was an important year for Fender. The first was the move to South Raymond Avenue, which took place in March. The old buildings in Pomona Avenue were by now bursting at the seams. In fine weather, which occupies much of the year in southern California, the crush could be eased by working outdoors, particularly on cabinet finishing. But rain made that impossible, and the factory did not meet fire and health regulations.

The new facility was to be built on the three-and-a-half acre site of a former orange ranch that Leo had acquired at the junction of S. Raymond Avenue and Valencia Drive. Three brand new buildings were initially erected on the site, which was large enough to permit expansion in the years to come: Leo insisted on building separate units in case he needed to divest himself of some of the space if things went wrong. He kept his own office and laboratory at South Pomona. The move took place in early spring, with heavy machinery being moved at weekends. Somehow no concrete or blacktop had been laid between the individual buildings, and that had to wait for drier weather. Typically, Leo's answer was to provide some foot-scrapers, but those who were there recall a muddy first spring.

TESTING THE STRAT The principal project at this time was the development of the Stratocaster guitar. In the words of Don Randall, "The Esquire and Telecaster are pretty ugly guitars when it comes right down to it. We needed a fancier guitar, an upgrade guitar." The Stratocaster with its three pickups, individual string bridges and vibrato system fitted the bill. Numerous people claim credit for some involvement in its design, notably Bill Carson, who began an association with Fender that continues to the present day.

Billy Carson, as he styled himself in those days, was a Western swing guitarist of some repute who started testing guitars and amplifiers for Leo on

BILLY CARSON uses *Fender* Electric Instruments

an informal basis some time in 1951. "Leo was quite pitch deaf, tone deaf. He really didn't have the faintest idea about music. But he had an uncanny ability to take your ideas and turn them into a manufactured end item." Carson bought a Telecaster but, he says "wanted a lot more than that instrument had to offer. I finally got Leo to build me one and we went on to put it into production: the Stratocaster."

Carson's testing role, which led to him formally joining the company in 1957, was not confined to new guitars. He had been informally testing amplifiers by both Magnatone and Fender but found himself caught in the crossfire between the two Southern California rivals. In the end, he opted for Fender, finding the Magnatone "a little bit sissy sounding".

Carson is clear about where to put the credit for creating new models. "The guy who called the shots in getting some things implemented and started was Don Randall. He would get around to the clubs and see guys like myself and get an opinion about what was needed and take it to Leo and Freddie [Tavares, of whom more later] and they'd start putting it together."

The amplifiers Carson took out with him were in a very early state of development. "There'd be masking tape with numbers, like ink-pen marks on the tape, to set the knobs by. The chassis would be hand-made, out of hot-rolled steel, maybe 12 gauge or 16 gauge, with no plating or anything like that. I would take it out and leave it in a club with somebody else for a week sometimes and get somebody else to listen to it to back up my own opinions as to how good or bad it was and what it needed. You hated like hell to see Leo coming. Irrespective of what you were in the middle of, a performance or playing a song or a tune, he had a way of grinning and walking right up and changing your amplifier settings while you were playing. He'd say 'Now, don't that sound better?' Nobody liked to see Leo coming in those days because he was a pest."

PLAYER INPUT In those innocent times there was no such thing as a research and development department, or a marketing department: "There was just a handful of musicians on the West Coast that were guitar players, that were pros, and Leo respected their word as to what was needed simply because they weren't looking for anything. They could be truthful to him. He developed relationships with people who would tell him the truth and he was very quick to shed folks who told him what they thought he wanted to hear just in order to get merchandise from him."

Fender had not been slow in realising the value of artists' endorsements in the promotion of new instruments and equipment. The experience with Jimmy Bryant had taught the company that. Don Randall now sought to put things on a more solid footing. "People were eager to use our instruments because they were just so far superior to anybody else's. But if I thought the people were valuable enough I would strike a deal with them and we would give them the instrument, but only to use. We retained the title.

"That came about because in the early days I put out a few instruments with guys. One of them, his name was Shifti Henry, and he proved to be just as the name implies. About every three months, he'd turn up and say, 'Oh man, somebody broke in my car and stole my instrument: I've got to have a new instrument.' A lot of these guys would take them out and hawk them. So we knocked that off. We maintained a hold on them after that. But then, for the use of the instruments we had the use of their names and pictures and all that stuff for our catalogues."

FENDER SALES By this time Randall's involvement in the Fender operation had deepened. The old R&TEC arrangement had been replaced by Fender Sales, based in Santa Ana, which was a four-way partnership between Leo, Randall, Francis Hall (owner of R&TEC) and Charlie Hayes, a salesman who had also previously worked for R&TEC.

This arrangement was not entirely satisfactory. Leo and Francis Hall "didn't hit it off", in Randall's words, and the result was a long period of niggling animosity. Then Charlie Hayes was killed in a head-on car accident in early 1955, not far from the factory in Raymond Avenue. Francis Hall left Fender after purchasing Rickenbacker. From that time on Fender Sales was jointly owned by Leo and Don Randall. Leo retained sole ownership and the presidency of the manufacturing arm, Fender Electric Instruments, and Randall became president of Fender Sales and various other subsidiaries, including a publishing company and a music teaching organisation.

Increasingly, Leo was relying on Freddie Tavares (left) for assistance in product development. Tavares was a Hawaiian-born musician, best known for

playing the steel guitar riff that starts off Warner Bros' Looney Tunes cartoons. A naturally modest man, he is held in great affection by everyone who knew him, which makes him virtually unique in the Fender story. Carson puts it like this: "Freddie contributed more to amplifier design than any other single person in the Fender company."

His first really important contribution was to help in salvaging the Stratocaster after initial problems with the tremolo unit. It had to be redesigned, and production was delayed. In a rare interview, conducted in 1979, Tavares said, "When it was just Leo and I we did what we pleased. In other words, Leo did what he pleased and I was just his assistant."

WHITE ON BOARD Leo's tendency to do what he pleased was to prove slightly troublesome as the company grew. An obsessive worker, he thought nothing of staying at his bench until late at night. At the same time, he expected to be able to intervene in the production process as much as he had in the days when there were only a handful of employees. But the S. Raymond Avenue factory was the start of the transition to becoming a large, professional organisation, and with rock'n'roll and the eventual success of the Stratocaster boosting the volume of manufacturing, things could not go on the way they had.

In spring 1954, Forrest White joined the company in a key role. He was an industrial engineer who had worked in aerospace in Akron, Ohio, before moving to California. Leo invited him to lunch and suggested he might be interested in helping to sort out some "management problems" at the new factory.

These turned out to revolve around what is now euphemistically known as "cash flow". "Freddie Tavares had told Leo that the company was ready to go down the drain, it was that bad," White told Tony Bacon in 1992. "He had no credit whatsoever, had to pay cash buying any material and so on. Some of the employees' cheques were bouncing. Freddie had said that Leo didn't have anyone in the plant that could do what needed to be done. So it just so happened that my timing was right."

White (right) found that the new premises, described in the local paper as "a beautiful new plant", were a mess. "There was no planning whatsoever, because Leo was not an engineer, he was an accountant. Things had just been set down any place."

He agreed to take charge, becoming plant manager. George Fullerton stayed on as production foreman, and initially there was some friction between the two men. White, with his background in production engineering, set about reorganising the plant, particularly in relation to the flow of parts and materials. Previously, production workers had wandered off to a bin in one of the more distant buildings to collect new components. When the bins were empty, more components were ordered. This was no longer appropriate in an era of rapidly growing production.

LEO & FORREST White joined the company on the understanding that he would have a free hand. That agreement was tested very rapidly. "Leo was a workaholic," said White. "He was just work, work, work. Things were pretty rough for him in the early days and he just worked like a demon. And I'll tell you something, he was always trying to perfect something.

"With those larger amps there was hardly any two production runs that were the same as far as the chassis was concerned. Leo would go round and he'd be working on something that he thought he'd change in the amplifier.

"Now I'd got the responsibility of running the plant. We'd maybe be using one resistor of one kind and 10 of another on an amplifier: he'd go in there and

change it. Maybe where the one was he'd use six of those and only two of the one where we were using 10 before. So the guy that was doing the testing, he'd wonder why he couldn't get his voltages to check out right, because all the voltages had been changed.

"So one day this guy, he says, 'Forrest, I've had it. I've been working on an amplifier chassis out there, trying to get it to check out for the last three hours, and I find out Leo's been at it again, changed it, and didn't say a thing.' I said, 'I'll take care of this.' So I put a notice on the bulletin board: 'Notice. Any employee making any kind of production change on assembly or otherwise, without previous authorisation from your immediate supervisor, is subject to immediate termination.' About 15 minutes later, Leo came into my office.

"He said, 'This is my company, you think I'd be able to do as I please.' I said 'You can Leo, fine, it's your responsibility now. You take it over. From now on I'm gonna do just what you want me to do, but buddy, it's not my responsibility, it's your responsibility. Now what do you want me to do first?' I said, 'Leo, if it's my responsibility, then it's going to have to be the way we agreed. If you take that sign down, then you run it, not me.' I didn't have any more problems with him."

SPEAK CLEARLY With the radical innovations in guitar design now out of the way, Leo turned back to amplifiers. The performance of his amplifiers was limited by the poor performance of contemporary speakers. In the Champions and other low-end amplifiers Fender would use whatever was available, but for its more expensive models the company turned to Jensen's hi-fidelity Concert series loudspeakers. These used AlNiCo magnets, made of an aluminium, nickel and cobalt alloy. AlNiCo was developed just before the war and made lightweight, permanent magnet speakers a possibility for the first time. The Jensen AlNiCo 5 speakers with distinctive blue dust caps are deemed to have almost magical qualities by collectors, especially since AlNiCo has been replaced almost entirely by ceramic materials in modern loudspeakers.

Even so, contemporary speaker technology was no match for the power output then being generated by Fender's amplifiers: the Super and then the Twin were by now leading the power race, producing about 15W each. All but the very tiniest amplifiers had now turned to paired output valves, working in what is called "push-pull" mode, where one valve amplifies the positive half of the signal and the other amplifies the negative half. This permits very efficient operation, giving high power output for low power consumption and keeping valve wear down, although some purists do not consider the sound as "sweet" as that produced by an amp in which the output valves amplify both halves of the wave form. But the speakers themselves were another problem. "I used to fight with these guys all the time," says Don Randall, "because they would say, 'We don't have this trouble with other manufacturers.' And I would say, 'No, you don't, because you are not working at the kind of power we are. You're putting them in radios and your ultimate listening power is probably only half to one-and-a-half Watts. That's probably all anybody can stand in a radio. You're just not understanding what's going on.' "

Eventually, changes were made to speaker design. Heavier and larger voice coils were able to handle more power, but the price was a loss of attack: the heavier voice coil simply did not respond as quickly as a light one. But that was later. For now, Fender looked at ways of compensating for poor transducer performance at both ends of the chain, principally by the use of tone controls and improved circuitry.

The early amplifiers had been based on the simplest designs culled from the valve manufacturers' manuals. They used metal-cased military valves of

obscure types. From the early 1950s, these were gradually replaced by modern, miniature type glass valves. Because they were smaller, more of these 12AX7 or 12AY7 types could occupy the same physical space. The extra valves could be used for another stage of amplification, increasing both the possibilities for overdrive distortion and ultimate volume, or for more sophisticated tone controls. It is worth remembering, though, that for most musicians and engineers at this time clean power and good tone was the aim, both because it was most appropriate to their music and because they would often expect their guitar amplifiers to provide perfectly clean amplification of vocal or accordion signals. The taste for distortion was a much later development.

The Twin, which had been introduced in 1952, benefited from most of the innovations first. From its introduction it included an extra stage of amplification between input and power amplifier. In successive variants, it gained separate bass and treble controls, a presence control, and a middle control: once pioneered on the Twin, they would be used elsewhere in the amplifier range. The presence control was a particular innovation. From now on, Fender power amp circuits used negative feedback, a device whereby some of the output is fed back to an earlier stage and used to reduce the stage's overall amplification, improving quality. In the presence circuit, high frequencies are excluded from this arrangement to a degree controlled by the presence pot.

Bill Carson has his own explanation for Leo Fender's electronic innovations. "I think this was born out of frugality: he was very frugal to the day he died. He would use a vacuum tube and if the voltage called for was 90 volts he'd use 110. He got the absolute maximum he could out of vacuum tube circuitry and design." Certainly it is the case that the valves were operated at voltages beyond those recommended as maximum in the design manuals. That tended to make them louder but reduced valve life.

FAB CABS The innovative aspects of the Fender designs were not solely inside the cabinet. An unusual amount of care went into the cabinets themselves. From the time of the tweed Champ, all were made of "finger-jointed" wood, either solid pine or ply. Leo knew musicians: he knew what would happen to his amplifiers out on the road and the search was always on to make them stronger. "Leo Fender would not build anything unless it was strong as a horse," noted Forrest White. The amplifiers were also designed to be serviceable. Leo's experience as a radio repairman made him develop a chassis structure that was held in place by metal straps but that could be swiftly removed for servicing. The chassis straps and the protective metal corners on the later Tolex amplifiers were made for Fender by Olmsted & Race, a local engineering firm. Karl Olmsted remembers Leo explaining why the amplifiers had to be tough. "He said, 'Well, these country & western cowboys, they put it in the back of the pickup and it bounces out on to the country road, you've got to have it so that you can pick it up, plug it back in and it still works some.' That chassis strap, when he first went to the expense of putting that on, people would say, 'Well, what are you putting that on for?' And that's why he did it.

"They'd drop them, and the top would be hanging on four screws. The heads would pop the way they used to make them, with just a washer, and pull out of the wood. And so Leo came up with the idea of what they called these chassis straps, which stopped that."

The final, and best loved, incarnation of the tweed amplifiers came in 1954: the "narrow panel" style, in which the speaker grille was expanded at top and bottom to leave only a narrow frame around it on all sides. These amplifiers are the most highly-prized by collectors

and players, especially the rare 3 x 10in Bandmaster of that year and the 4 x 10in Bassman, which shared effectively the same chassis and circuitry.

The single 15in speaker with which the Bassman had started had proved too fragile, with fundamental notes from the Precision Bass pushing its voice coil and cone beyond their normal travel to destructive effect. The 1959 5F6A version of this amplifier, with four input sockets, a middle control, different output valves and 40W power output, is probably the most desired vintage amp in the world. It has recently been marketed by Fender in their reissues series.

Don Randall always wanted new models, or a new look, for the annual trade shows. "It wasn't necessarily demand," he says, "Perhaps that entered into it, who knows? But it was more a marketing ploy on our part to get more and more amplifiers and more models on to the market. It's like the car companies: if you buy a General Motors car you can get a Pontiac, an Oldsmobile, a Chevrolet, a Cadillac and so on." While the principal improvements were output power and different speaker arrangements, other innovations were always welcome. "You had to have something new or you were losing ground," says Randall.

BASSMAN

To many collectors and players, the narrow-panel "four-hole" Bassman is the classic guitar amplifier.

The narrow panel tweed Bassman represents the final stages of the evolution of the combo version of this amplifier. Although they all look approximately the same, there are pronounced differences in the circuitry of the versions produced each year between 1954 and 1959. The final 5F6A version, which connects its negative feedback loop to the phase inverter, is the most prized.

Earlier versions of the narrow-panel Bassman had only two input sockets. The more collectible versions 5F6 and 5F6A add two more sockets and a middle control. The version number is usually on the 'tube chart' label, inside the back of the cabinet.

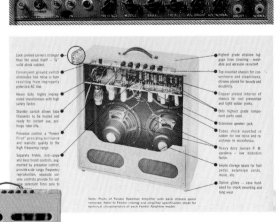

Fender's catalogues (above) placed great emphasis on engineering. Four speakers were more reliable than one had been.

In 1955, that something new was tremolo, the rhythmic fluctuation of volume, which had previously been heard in home organs and was now introduced by Leo to his amplifier range with the Tremolux, a simple 15W amp with a single 12in speaker. A single 12AX7 valve was used as an oscillator,

providing a fluctuating supply of current to one of the amplifying valves imparting the characteristic throbbing to the sound output. This use of the valve meant, however, that its output, at 15W, was lower than other amplifiers with a comparable number of valves. An even lower-powered version, the Vibrolux, appeared in 1956. It used its modest complement of four valves even more economically, by using half the first valve to provide oscillation for the tremolo circuit rather than for amplification. Its output was 10W, into a single 10in speaker. Fender also introduced the five-valve Harvard amplifier with an 8in speaker at $99.50.

TREMOLUX

The Tremolux introduced tremolo to the Fender amplifier range, but at the expense of output power.

Tremolo, a rhythmic fluctuation of volume, had been used in home organs before Fender introduced it to its amplifier line in the Tremolux. But using one of the amplifier's 12AX7 twin-triode valves to produce the effect meant that, at 15W, the Tremolux was less powerful than it might have been.

The Vibrolux was the Tremolux's smaller sibling, using four amplifier valves to produce 10W into a single 10in speaker.

The Tremolux came in a cabinet as big as the Pro's and had as many valves as the Super, but was less powerful than either. This was not a winning combination and it was later remodelled as a 30W amplifier in piggy-back style.

At the other end of the price scale, Fender introduced in late 1958 a new guitar, the Jazzmaster ($329.50 on introduction) which was soon accompanied by another new product, the Vibrasonic amplifier ($479.50). This broke new ground in two ways. It used a JB Lansing speaker and it had a new type of cabinet and covering, a cloth-backed vinyl called Tolex. The cabinet featured a front-facing control panel: it was protected by a patent, applied for in June 1959.

TOLEX Bill Carson recalls trying a prototype of a new type of JBL speaker using a copper-wound voice-coil instead of the usual aluminium. Coupled with a light paper speaker cone it was supposed to provide more bite for guitar, but it couldn't handle the power required: it broke up. The Vibrasonic used a standard heavy-duty JBL speaker which some found harsh. It was not an outstanding success. But its covering, manufactured by the General Tire & Rubber Company of Akron, Ohio, was soon to become the standard for amplifier use. It was easy to work and could take a lot of abuse on the road, although the early cream and tan colours were less forgiving in that respect than the later black.

VIBRASONIC

The Fender Vibrasonic broke new ground in several ways. But this design was not equipped for long-term survival.

For the Vibrasonic of 1959, Leo Fender introduced several innovations, starting with a new cabinet and front panel design. A patent application of 1958 shows the new cabinet, sloping away at the top front. It does not show the new Tolex covering, a kind of cloth-backed vinyl acquired from U.S. Tyre & Rubber of Akron, Ohio. The first Tolex was in a coarse-textured brown. Cream and black versions came later. The Vibrasonic used a 15in speaker acquired from J. B. Lansing. Its electronics and chassis were shared with the Pro Amp.

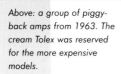

Above: a group of piggy-back amps from 1963. The cream Tolex was reserved for the more expensive models.

Although the Vibrasonic was essentially a Pro with a tremolo circuit and a JBL speaker, it did require a new chassis design to accommodate for the first time a front-facing control panel. This feature, too, was extended across the range. But the Vibrasonic's place at the top of the range was short-lived. It was soon usurped by the Showman, first of the piggy-back amplifiers, in which the electronics were contained in one slim cabinet sitting on top of a larger speaker enclosure. The Showman was a response to new, higher powered amplifiers from other manufacturers and shared a chassis with the Twin, which now was capable of about 85W output. The Showman's separate speaker cabinet contained either a 12in or 15in JBL unit. The Bandmaster, Bassman and Tremolux were converted to piggy-back style at the same time.

REVERB The remaining technical innovation of these years was reverberation. Created by passing signal into a transducer, vibrating a spring, and then converting those spring vibrations back into sound, it was first used in home organs for a churchy effect. It made its debut in the Fender line as

SHOWMAN

The Fender Showman was the first amplifier in piggy-back style.
It remains a popular choice with collectors.

The Showman was introduced in 1961 at the head of the Fender range. By using separate enclosures for amplifier and loudspeaker it attempted to tackle the increasing problem of portability. The two can be locked together, and the speaker cabinet, which houses a 12in or 15in J.B.L. driver, can be tilted back and supported on its own legs. The Dual Showman is the same amp with a 2 x 15in speaker cabinet.

Fender's elaborate catalogues always emphasized the technical innovations and manufacturing quality of the new amplifiers.

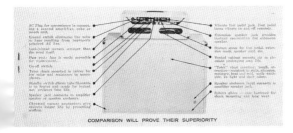

COMPARISON WILL PROVE THEIR SUPERIORITY

a separate item, using a spring bought from Hammond, from 1961. It was first incorporated in an amplifier with the Vibroverb of 1963 and then spread widely throughout the amp line, just as vibrato/tremolo had before it.

By now the amplifier line had come a very long way from its simple wooden-boxed beginnings. With the extension of black tolex to cover everything,

and its associated blackface front panels, the amplifiers had reached their final pre-CBS form. Internally, too, they had come a long way. Most now included two channels with separate tone controls on each, plus vibrato/ tremolo and reverberation. Power output had grown enormously since the early days. The hand-assembled look and feel of the early equipment was replaced by the slick mass produced appearance of the blackface amps.

Of course, by modern standards, this was hardly mass production.

REVERB UNIT

The Fender Reverb Unit used a reverberation spring provided by the Hammond organ company to provide a new sound for guitarists and singers.

The Reverb Unit, introduced in 1961, works by turning the electrical signal into vibrations in a spring and then back again with added "twang". Three valves are used in the process, providing a considerable gain boost. Units came in all three Tolex colours.

The numbers were high (Don Randall recalls ordering anything up to 50,000 speakers in a year) but huge numbers of variants were permitted, as Fender's engineers accommodated different suppliers and component specifications, not to mention Leo's own innovations. Fender's catalogues of the time warned buyers that specifications were likely to change without notice and they weren't joking. Thus these amps now attract collectors and obsessives, quite irrespective of their merits as sound reproducers, which are considerable.

OPTIMISM The guitar boom of the late 1950s and early 1960s placed Fender in a prime position. It had already grown a long way. The three new buildings of 1953 were immediately joined by a fourth. Two more were added in 1956, the same year Leo bought his first yacht. Three more units arrived in 1959: the original site was now full. So was Fender's order book. With endorsement by prominent artists (of all those in the catalogues of the day, only the Beach Boys are still with us) and a reliable, saleable range of products the future looked bright. Unfortunately, difficult times were just around the corner.

TWIN REVERB

The Fender Twin Reverb, particularly in its pre-CBS blackface version, has long been a favourite amplifier with the working musician for its power and compactness.

The blackface look is seen at its best in this Fender Twin Reverb of 1964. Capable of about 80W from four 6L6 output valves, the amp was powerful enough for most club gigs and has an excellent sound.

Cover stars: The Twin Reverb and the Jaguar guitar on the 1963/64 catalogue.

Why did Leo Fender sell his company? This is a question that many people have tried to answer but the decision seems to have its roots in Leo's peculiar psychology. His obsessive nature was apparent from his endless tinkering with apparently successful products and his long working hours. With the company operating smoothly, he had time to turn that obsessive interest in on himself, in particular by devoting ever more attention to his own health. He had long been a fanatic about diet, experimenting with various vegetable juices and encouraging his long-suffering employees to do the same.

He explained his health problems in a 1980 interview with BAM magazine. "In 1955, I got a strep infection in my sinus, and several times a year I'd have to go over to the doc and get a penicillin or streptomycin shot. It would keep leaking from the sinus down over the palate and over the throat, so every time I'd get around a cold breeze I'd get strep throat again."

This was a debilitating, uncomfortable condition, though not normally a life threatening one. But Leo had become convinced that he had not long to live. According to Don Randall, Leo asked him if he would like to buy him out for a million-and-a-half dollars. Randall declined, but told Leo he would look for an outside buyer. Negotiations were opened with Baldwin Piano & Organ Co of Ohio, but fell through. Leo rejected another suggestion, that the company go public. Eventually a firm of investment bankers hired by Randall came up with the name of the Columbia Broadcasting System.

CBS TAKE OVER CBS was at that time one of the biggest corporations in the country, with a turnover of more than $500 million a year, and a vast range of interests. It had just bought the New York Yankees baseball team and was constantly on the lookout to diversify. From its citadel in New York, CBS must have viewed Fender as just the kind of undercapitalised, undermanaged company that would benefit from big city know-how and finance: as a broadcaster, it had seen the tremendous impact that the Beatles and other new artists were having on America's youth.

After protracted negotiations taking up much of 1964, CBS offered $13m for the firm. Leo had left everything in Don Randall's hands and made himself

scarce. "He wouldn't even talk to the principals," says Randall, "And when we closed the sale he wouldn't go back to New York for the closing. He didn't want any part of it." CBS president Goddard Lieberson announced on signing, "This is a fast growing business tied into the expanding leisure time market. We expect this industry will grow by 23 per cent in the next two years."

CBS had hired experts to investigate the company fully before the sale went through, in January 1965. They must have been satisfied with what they

had acquired, even though it was by far the highest price ever paid for a
musical instrument manufacturer. For their money they got a company
employing about 750 people in a complex of nine buildings at South Raymond
Avenue and anything up to 20 other properties elsewhere in the area, with plans
for a new factory building of some 120,000 sq ft well advanced. They got an
order book worth about $9m and Fender's entire existing management team.

Randall became vice-president and general manager of Fender Electrical
Instrument Co, Inc and Fender Sales, Inc, now known as the Fender Musical
Instruments division of Columbia Records Distribution Corporation, itself part of
the Columbia Broadcasting System. Forrest White continued to run the plant, at
least initially, although he lost the "vice-president and general manager" title he
had held since the instrument company's 1959 incorporation. He also says his
salary dropped to one-third of what it had been. Leo, for his part, signed an
agreement that made him a consultant to CBS for five years and required him
to desist from going into business in competition for a further five years.

CULTURE CLASH Don Randall had hired Paul Spranger, an
electronics engineer with a background in aerospace, to be the new director of
research and development and to take charge of Fender's lab. Leo was given his
own workshop in a different location. "They put him and his staff down in a
building a couple of blocks away from the main building and virtually isolated
him," recalls Bill Carson. "They wouldn't use any of his ideas until later on when
they found out how good a lot of those ideas were."

Amp and guitar collectors have long made a fetish of the distinction
between pre-CBS and CBS-era instruments and amplifiers, with the latter
representing everything bad. In this they have received plenty of support from
those who were there at the time. "CBS?" says Bill Carson, "Oh yes, we lived
through that nightmare." But mythology aside, there was no overnight
deterioration: workforce, materials and designs changed only gradually. It is to
CBS's credit that they wanted to build the Fender company up, rather than
simply cashing in on its assets. They wanted, above all, to increase production
to meet demand for electric instruments which was then at its height. To do so
they employed experts in high-volume production and engineers with college
degrees. The result was a clash of cultures with the existing staff and
management, who were by and large long-serving craft-workers without formal
qualifications who had grown with the company.

"CBS was a well-intentioned company," says Bill Carson. "And like many
large corporations they had a deep hip-pocket to do a lot of research and
development. But it was so systematised. They had systems on us that would
have fitted General Motors."

QUALITY CONTROL Interestingly, some of CBS's new recruits
were production engineers from the automobile industry. Paul Rivera, who
helped revive Fender in the early 1980s, blames them for starting the rot. "The
CBS boys in New York said, 'These country bumpkins down in Orange County,
what do they know? Let's bring in some guys from Ford who really understand
volume production.' And that's when quality control really went down the toilet.

I ran into old memos from the people back in '66, '67, '68, and one of them stated that back in Ford they allowed the dealers to do the repairs on new products. They were part of the quality, not control but reparation process. They sent out shoddy merchandise to their dealers, knowing that the dealers would fix it for their customers, so it wasn't required for them to have such high quality control!"

FINGER JOINT Leo never admitted there had been a collapse in quality. Don Randall, who remained with the company for five years, takes a similar view. "I will just say this for CBS," he told Tony Bacon in 1992, "They were just as interested in quality as we were. They spared no amount of time or effort to ensure that quality was there."

Of course, Randall was running the company on CBS's behalf at that time: the view from the other end of the pecking order looks different. Sam Hutton worked on the cabinet production line and saw work rushed. "They used the box joint: we call it a finger joint because it's like putting your fingers together. It should have three surfaces glued: if you put your fingers together you've got the sides to each finger and the end where it bottoms out. All the cabinets would have been very good if that had been done correctly.

"Except that the way we did them rather shattered the wood. We worked so fast there were actually hollow places where you could see through. If it's done correctly, you can't see anything, but in the Fender cabinets you can look inside and see where they are shattered, so that it's not as strong as it should be."

The problems with the cabinets were just one way in which the dash for growth manifested itself. Karl Olmsted, co-owner of Race & Olmsted, the engineering shop that had supplied many of Fender's machined parts for both guitars and amplifiers from the early days, blames the growth in production more than he blames CBS for any drop in quality. "The quality never went down as much as some people say. It did deteriorate a little bit, but that was not because CBS bought them but because their production was going up so fast. It's like any other business in the world, you can't increase production that much without sacrificing quality."

CBS ACCOUNTS By the end of the first year of CBS's ownership, output had increased by 80 per cent over the 1964 figure, according to a letter from Don Randall to Forrest White. He told White he and his workers had done "a remarkable job". But CBS's attempt to impose its corporate ways on to the ingrained Fender culture was only just beginning. In June 1966, Fender Musical Instruments was renamed the CBS Musical Instrument Division, with Don Randall as president. White was named Director of Manufacturing, although he insists neither his pay nor his duties changed.

One of CBS's methods was internal accounting, the division of all activities into cost-centres "down to the last nut, bolt and screw" in Randall's words, that produced reams of paper and slowed decision making to a crawl. These figures would eventually be used to distribute overheads around the companies in the CBS musical instrument group, several of which were less efficient than Fender. In time that became a nightmarish problem for management.

Corporate thinking was behind another plan, to rewrite all the workers' job descriptions, something that introduced petty demarcation disputes into an area which had previously been free of them. And all parties recall office politics being played out on a grand scale between California and New York. Forrest White once said, "CBS had a vice president for everything. I think they had a vice-president for cleaning the toilets." And Don Randall concurs: "Everybody at CBS was climbing the corporate ladder, stepping on everyone else's fingers."

"They were a lot of outsiders who didn't know what we were doing and had nothing to gain by doing well," says Sam Hutton. "CBS spent more time fighting the employees who were trying to do a good job than they did developing a product."

Musicians had always been attracted to work for Fender, because it seemed like a good area to work to supplement their musical earnings. Constantly, there were always players on hand to test and improve the product. The new people did not share this background. They were professional engineers and professional managers, but to people like Hutton they were

"amateurs". He recalls a piece of gossip at the time. "Somebody said if you worked for CBS in New York and you were a bad boy they sent you to Fullerton. It seemed like that. We had a constant turnover of incompetent management.

"I turned in hundreds and hundreds of suggestions [mainly for ways to strengthen the cabinets] and I could manage to get to the people who had the power, but in every case these people seemed like they were exhausted. They couldn't listen any more or were doing two jobs and they didn't know what to do."

The new engineers were no more popular than the managers. Most of the existing Fender people were musicians with a working understanding of electronics: the new breed were people with an education but with less practical understanding of what working musicians wanted. Some came from the growing aerospace world, some straight from college. "They hired people who had degrees in theoretical physics," says Hutton, perhaps not the most reliable witness. "It was a buddy system. If you went to college with the man who just happened to be running the place at the time, the chances are you got a job."

DISTORTED VIEW This clash of outlooks came to a head when the time came to introduce some radical new amplifier models. Initially, CBS kept all the existing models going without changes, but the temptation to modify the existing product was strong. Looked at from our own time, it is easy to say that one of the principal requirements of a guitar amplifier is that it distort, easily and pleasingly. Seen from the perspective of an electronic engineer working in 1965, things looked very different.

Audio engineers spend all their time striving to remove distortion. The early Fender amps were never intended to distort, but the limitations of their valves meant that if you turned them up full they would "clip". Musicians in some fields found this pleasing, though it had no appeal for others who simply wanted more clean power. CBS's engineers sought ways of making the amplifiers more powerful, more stable in performance, and less inclined to distort. The fact that this removed many of their more appealing characteristics is something that is only obvious with the benefit of hindsight.

JAMAICAN RESISTORS One particular area of controversy is the introduction of solid state silicon rectifiers. These have all of solid state's advantages, and because they are only in the power supply and not in the signal path, you might have thought they would be universally approved of as something better. Not so. Unlike the valve rectifiers they replaced, silicon rectifiers do not cause the supply voltage they produce to drop when they are being driven hard. The result is a tighter, punchier sound: but it lacks a particular quality, of almost organic interaction, that valve purists claim exists in the original valve-rectified product. Because a valve rectifier allows the voltage it supplies to "sag", it tends to reduce the attack of a loud note and then increase the volume as the note fades: a kind of compression is introduced that some find attractive. This type of entirely subjective effect makes an objective consideration of amplifier design entirely impossible: so much is, undeniably, simply a matter of taste.

There were, on the other hand, less nobly intentioned reasons for the changes: ease of manufacture and cheapness. Here there was great potential for inadvertent damage. Some ex-Fender employees talk of cheap Jamaican resistors and electrolytic capacitors that, instead of being built into aluminium cans, as is usual, were in moulded plastic cases. "The buyers were just buying to save money and impress the boss," said one engineer, " 'Look at this, I got resistors for half the price!' Nobody gave a shit." Later, when attempts were made to use printed circuit boards as a cheaper and easier replacement for the traditional "point to point" wiring of components, whole new areas of difficulty and controversy were opened up.

TRANSISTOR TRAIN-WRECK The clash between new and old in both personnel and methods came to a head with the development of Fender's first transistor amplifiers in the mid-1960s. This was an opportunity for the new breed of engineers to show what they could do. It was a disaster that would have destroyed a less dominant company – "a train-wreck" in the words of one later engineer.

At the time, solid state electronics were relatively new and were seen as having all the advantages. They were small, light, ran at low voltages and used little power, promised to last for ever and to produce less distortion than valve circuitry. They were also the exciting new technological development of the day. As Don Randall puts it, in an echo of the era, "If you shoot a man to the moon you couldn't do it with tubes. Tubes are a very inefficient form of amplifying the sound that you create. You have a filament in there, a cathode that heats up. You have a lot of heat generated and you have a lot of pieces in there that will vibrate, bang around, cause feedback. They are just a very inefficient type of thing, when you think you can do the same thing with a little chip on a plate: you can develop a lot more power in a lot smaller space with a lot less weight and practically no heat created."

Unfortunately, it was not to prove as simple as CBS had hoped. The new owner of Fender could see a threat from other manufacturers who were introducing solid state equipment and brought in engineers to head it off. One was Bob Rissi, who moved up from the repair centre to work on the first Fender solid state amps. He still defends them.

"Things were pretty heavy there, because Vox were coming out with their new [solid state] product and Thomas Organ [maker of the entirely separate US Vox amplifiers] was putting out their solid state. They were taking one attitude to design and we were taking a totally different one. In a way theirs was more successful.

"It wasn't as producible by any means, but they were interested in designing a sound that people were looking for. We were more interested in designing a sound that we felt would sell just because Fender put it out as something new. It worked for some people, but not for others. I knew that it was going to happen, but other people in the company felt that if Fender put it out it 'created' a sound. If felt like, you're better off creating what musicians want."

SOLID STATE The amplifiers were first presented to Forrest White, who was going to have to build them, in September 1966. They

numbered 14 in total, in new cabinets of considerable ugliness. The supposed solid state advantage of compactness had been sacrificed to vulgar display, and to add insult to the traditionalists' injuries, they bore identical names to the long running valve amps. There was a Solid State Bassman, Solid State Twin Reverb and so on. One innovation was the "style" switch, which allowed players to choose between pop, normal, and "CW/RR".

White took the view that they were designed neither for easy production nor for servicing in the field. After prevaricating for a while, and failing to make contact with Don Randall to raise his objections, White was threatened with replacement. So, on December 6, 1966, he resigned, telling his colleagues that he had done so out of respect for the good name of Leo Fender.

Some have doubted White's version of events, suggesting that he had fallen foul of an efficiency drive, but Sam Hutton, who had negotiated with him as a production line union representative (Fender workers had founded their own house union in the late 1950s), backs him up. "Forrest has told me this several times, that he knew the solid state amps were not ready but the CBS management insisted they be put into production. He was simply told, either you'll sign them into production or we'll put somebody in your job that will. And he lost his job."

Production went ahead, and proved as difficult as White had predicted. There were problems getting them built in a factory that had never worked with printed circuit boards or delicate low-temperature components. Many of those which were sold, starting in late 1967, came quickly back to the factory. According to Rissi, "A guy who took over from me in repairs said they were coming back partly because of manufacturing, not the design."

Some but not all. Even Rissi admits that "it didn't meet the sound requirements of people who'd been listening to valve amps, with distortions, all these years and all of a sudden they have this pure solid state sound." It was, of course, typical of Fender's luck in these years that it had decided to introduce a new and uncannily clean sound at a time when musicians like Hendrix (who used a fuzzbox with his Twin) and Jeff Beck were exploring distortion.

SOLDER But even those who did like the sound, and there were some, especially among bass players and those who were using the PA version, had problems with the equipment. Rissi: "It was a matter of people on the line really not wanting to go to solid state using new production methods, flow solder and stuff." Flow solder was a technique whereby components would be mounted on a board and then the lower side of the board dipped in molten solder to make the connections. It promised to be very much faster than the old method of wiring every component to every other component by hand. "They feared for their jobs, because they thought you could produce much quicker with new techniques.

Fender's 1968 export catalogue (above) shows solid state versions of the Super Reverb, Twin Reverb and Pro Reverb in a sylvan setting. Giving the new amps the same names as their valve forebears did nothing for their popularity.

This British leaflet for the Solid State Bassman (left), produced by the importer, Arbiter, shows a different speaker cabinet to that seen in contemporary American catalogues, with a traditional badge on the grille. The Bassman was the only solid-state amp to achieve any kind of success.

'SOLID STATE' SERIES BASSMAN AMPLIFIER

Fender

Fully transistorised

2×12" exclusive heavy duty Lansing speakers

100w.(British) output

arbiter ltd

Rec. retail price 277Gns

It wasn't that they were doing it on purpose, but the training that was done. I don't think people were giving it the attention that they should.

"The first ones that went out were actually manufactured with things missing or put in wrong. The way it was designed, it just so happened that they would work that way for a while before they'd overheat and blow up. A whole bunch of them got sent out and we got them back in and we'd find the defects. There were things like transistors put in upside down where they'd bent the legs and they would still fit. But they were shorting against a heatsink that happened to be black anodised. Eventually they would get hot enough, one of the legs would short and wipe out the circuit board or the transistor.

"A bunch of them got out that way because people didn't pay attention to putting transistors in the right way. Power transistors have to be pulled up with screws on heatsinks. And when they were corrected those amps lasted a long time unless they were directly shorted on the output." More problems followed

Solid-State front panel design.

The 1969 Fender catalogue boasted of the compactness of the solid state chassis (below).

Solid-State component layout showing mini-aturization and chassis compactness.

The controls of the Solid State Deluxe Reverb (above) are reassuringly conventional, unlike the design of the aluminium front panel.

The complete solid state instrument amp range pictured at the 1968 Teenage Fair in Hollywood, California.

TWIN REVERB

The silverface version of the long-running amplifier has never been popular with collectors but it is a good workhorse.

Initially, the silverface version of the Twin Reverb was little different to its blackface predecessors. Later it received a master volume control and distortion switch and gave a higher power output. Various modifications were made to the circuitry: lately there has been a vogue for returning silverface Twins to blackface specifications.

Several Fender amps incorporated tilt-back legs for extra sound dispersion.

DUAL SHOWMAN REVERB

In its silverface version the Dual Showman Reverb continued to develop as a piggy-back version of the Twin.

The Dual Showman Reverb piggy-back amp was coupled with two 15in JBL speakers in a cabinet that made roadies weep.

The silverface look was extended right across the amplifier range, as this shot from the 1969 catalogue shows.

BASSMAN

The Bassman piggy-back amp – though not its speaker cabinet – remained unchanged for more than a decade.

The only significant change in the Bassman from 1964 to its demise at the end of the 1970s was a change from 12in speakers to 15in.

Blackface and silverface Bassmans have the same controls. In 1972 the silverface Bassman was renamed the Bassman 50.

over the choice of circuit board. Rissi selected a high quality glass fibre board but was over-ruled in favour of something that was cheaper but which apparently bent or cracked under the heat involved in the flow soldering process. There would be echoes of this story much later.

SILVERFACE Friction between the lab and the factory did not help with the manufacturing problems. Having worked in valve testing as well as in the lab, Rissi saw both sides. "I agreed with some of the guys who had been building valve amps as to why they thought things needed to stay this way. But I could also see that the new stuff we were designing in the lab was going to be great once it got filtered into the line." Bill Carson was unimpressed with the whole solid state adventure. "It was disastrous. It didn't look good, it didn't sound good. Hell, there was very little you could say about the entire line." He says the PA version was "fair". "If you needed a paging system for a big bus station it was pretty good."

The range lasted only about two years. Legend has it that the death knell was sounded when Don Randall was at a trade show in Europe and found himself unable to change a panel light on one of the amps without performing major surgery. Fender attempted to divert attention by restyling its valve amp range. These now sported an aluminium front panel and turquoise block lettering. The high power amplifiers, the Showman and Twin Reverb, now boasted an output of 85W from four 6L6 output valves. Despite being largely the same as the blackface amplifiers which immediately preceded them, these "silverface" amplifiers have never had the same collector appeal, which makes them a comparatively economical choice for the working musician. The style lasted until the reintroduction of the blackface look at the end of the 1970s.

SOLID STATE LOVER The solid state experiment was not over, however. In 1967 the legendary Gibson engineer Seth Lover (left) came to Fender to join his former boss Dick Evans, who had gone from the chief engineer's post

at Gibson to join Fender. Lover produced a number of innovative designs for Fender, including a guitar with built in effects including frequency dividing and doubling and an automatic wah-wah sound. It didn't go into production, unlike his Super Showman solid state amplifier. This was an ingenious amplifier that combined a 140W power amplifier built into a cabinet with either four 12in or eight 10in speakers and a separate three-channel pre-amplifier. "The salesmen down in the front office decided they had to have a three channel amplifier so that small groups could all play. But that never works, because the guy who owns an amplifier doesn't want anyone else plugging into it," recalls Lover.

Lover had built solid state fuzz boxes at Gibson, modelled on a faulty amplifier that had developed an interestingly distorted sound. For his Fender amplifier he applied this expertise. One channel had normal tone controls, a second had vibrato and reverb, what Lover scathingly calls "oil-can echo", and a third channel, for bass, had a fuzz tone and what the catalogue calls

"Dimension IV". Fender's sales force was still obsessed with the idea of selling it for three people to play through at once. Lover wanted to hedge his bets. "I told them I thought it would be a good idea if they put a switch on the back so that the lead guitar player could use any of the effects that were available to the other channels. They didn't want to do that.

"Then they got requests from the buyers who had bought the thing, and they still wouldn't put the switch on, but they got me to make jumper cords to jump from one channel to the other so that all the effects could be used."

The amp sold reasonably well, but like previous solid state efforts, was utterly unreliable. It had been dogged by the same manufacturing problems that had done for the earlier series. "The problem was that they were not very good at building solid state equipment. They wouldn't clean up the solder machine. We'd make a run of 50, I'd built them a test rig for testing them out, and 45 out of 50 would crap out. A problem was that they would never tighten down the bolts on the power transistors. The darn things would overheat and blow."

CAPRICORN

The Capricorn combo of 1970 had three 12in JBL speakers and an output of 105W. But it was no more successful than the rest of the Zodiac series, which rapidly disappeared.

The failure of the first solid state Fender instrument amplifiers did not deter CBS from trying again. The new Zodiac series, named after the star signs, sugared the solid state pill by combining conventional cabinets with expensive JBL speakers. No-one was convinced.

Exactly the same problems bedevilled the second full solid state range, the Zodiac series, which appeared in the same year, 1970. Each amplifier had a Zodiac name, Libra, Scorpio and so on: presumably someone thought it was the dawning of the age of Aquarius. These ill-starred amps at least had the virtue of looking more like conventional amplifiers, in that they were housed in similar cabinets and had unflashy valve-style control panels. The inclusion of expensive JBL speakers, honoured with their own badge on the grille cloth, should have made them more attractive but didn't. And reliability was as bad as ever. The line lasted just a year, after which their JBL speakers and grille cloth were distributed to other models.

THE BASS END Experimentation continued, but it tended to represent variations on the long-term Fender valve-amp themes. A great deal of effort went into broadening the bass amp range. The entry level Bantam Bass coupled a cut-down Bassman amplifier with a curious trapezoidal speaker with

400PS

The 400PS bass was one of Fender's more bizarre efforts. A giant 440W RMS valve amplifier using 13 valves drove a single 18in speaker in a folded-horn cabinet of frightening efficiency.

By the early 1970s it had long been apparent that many bass players would not be satisfied with what were really just oversized guitar combos. The 400PS was Fender's first attempt to address the problem of building a purpose-designed bass rig.

a plastic cone bought in from Yamaha. At the other end of the scale, the astonishing 400 PS of 1970 coupled three separate 145W valve amplifiers,

totalling 13 valves, with a huge 18in speaker in a folded horn cabinet of radical design.

The chassis of the Twin Amp, putting out 100W by 1972, was coupled with four 12in or six 10in speakers to produce the Quad Reverb and Super Six Reverb combos. And then the power race really started to get out of hand. "There was a period there when we really tried to strong arm everybody by overbuilding the output so that we got a lot more horsepower than the speakers would take," says Bill Carson.

An all-new product designed to meet this trend was the Super Twin of 1976, which used no fewer than six 6L6 output valves to produce 180W. A new,

The Quad Reverb (left) was one of a whole series of amps built around the Twin Reverb chassis.

SUPER SIX REVERB

Following the disaster of solid state, Fender's fortunes were revived with a series of heavyweight valve combos, one of which was the 100W Super Six Reverb.

Neither the Quad Reverb nor the Super Six Reverb is ever likely to win an award for elegance. Both used the same chassis, that of the Twin Reverb, which was providing 100W RMS by the early 1970s. The difference was in speaker complement: the Quad Reverb uses 4 x 12in drivers, the Super Six 6 x 10in. Castors (detachable on the Super Six) did something to ease the formidable mobility problems. Not recommended for buskers.

and rather unappealing, rendition of the classic blackface look was developed for this model. It surrounded a black grille cloth with a silver metal frame. It was a harbinger of things to come. By the beginning of the 1980s, Fender would revert to the blackface look for its entire line (purists can tell the difference simply by the fact that the Fender badge is not underlined) which suggested a company forced to look back to find its identity rather than forward.

In doing so, it would not have had much assistance from the old guard. Forrest White was the first to go, in 1967. Don Randall left CBS/Fender in April 1969. George Fullerton left a year later, and Leo ended his association with the company as soon as his contract permitted. Dale Hyatt, who had come back from running the radio shop and into the factory in the late 1950s, left CBS in 1972. Interestingly enough, once released from their CBS obligations, all continued to be involved in musical instrument and amplifier companies, providing yet more competition for a Fender organisation which had lost its way. New blood and new ideas were needed.

SUPER TWIN

The Super Twin of 1976 marked the high point of the power race.
It produced 180W from six 6L6 output valves

The Super Twin, marketed as "the new tube amp that travels light and comes on heavy", was a product of the Ed Jahns era at Fender. It achieved excellent laboratory performance but never won the affection of players. It introduced a new look, a step back in the direction of blackface but using black grille cloth with a white plastic surround.

ender's advertising characterised
he Super Twin as a kind of baboon,
nore noisy than clever.

By the late 1970s, the leadership that Fender had once held in the amplifier market had been squandered. On the mass market level, the pioneering

American company was slugging it out with newcomers such as Yamaha, Peavey and Roland, whose ultra-clean Jazz Chorus amplifier had introduced an appealing new sound. Don Randall's own company had achieved some success with solid state designs, mainly by developing a transistor output stage that mimicked the workings of a valve design. The Music Man amplifiers developed by Forrest White, after he had left CBS, used a hybrid design featuring transistors except in the final output.

NOT A FENDER In valve amplifier design, a number of smaller, more adaptable companies than the CBS-owned Fender were able to introduce important innovations by listening closely to what musicians wanted. Certainly few of these manufacturers shared Fender's early distaste for distortion. Instead, efforts were made to find ways of providing players with that sound at all output levels, rather than letting it arise accidentally when the amplifier was working hard. Ironically, the most important of these small companies, MESA Engineering, started in a way that depended entirely on Fender.

Randall Smith, who started the company, earned his reputation by shoe-horning a 60W Fender Bassman 4 x 10in amplifier chassis into the cabinet of a 12W Fender Princeton, equipping it with a 12in JBL speaker, and then reassembling the whole thing so it looked like Fender's original budget amplifier. The result had considerable appeal as a "wolf in sheep's clothing". But it wasn't just a novelty product. Championed by Carlos Santana for its powerful overdrive sound, Smith's amp achieved considerable acclaim. Smith was then working in a music shop and was able to order the output transformers and other parts he needed from Fender as spares. He built more than 200 of the amplifiers before Fender got wise and cut off the supply, by which time he was ready to produce an amplifier of his own.

MASTER VOLUME The MESA Boogie amplifier that Smith produced from 1972 introduced the master volume control. Rather than making each stage of the pre-amplifier produce exactly the level of signal required by the following stage, as you would if you wanted clean sound, he arranged things so that each stage was easily capable of overdriving the next. The master volume control sat between the pre-amp and the power amp. The right level of overdrive could then be set by the first volume control, and the appropriate sound then passed on to the power amplifier at a level set by the master volume control. Modern amplifiers have extended this technique so that there may well be three or more separate volume knobs in order to provide maximum control of overdrive.

Fender amplifiers designed with the intention that several players would use them at once, notably Seth Lover's ill-fated Super Showman, had featured master volume controls: this was simply so that balance could be achieved between the different instruments by the channel volume controls and then an overall sound level set. But from 1972/3, master volume controls were fitted to a number of Fender's amps with an explanation in the catalogue that it "lets you add any desired degree of distortion". Marshall, fast becoming Fender's most important competition, adopted the master volume system in 1975, by which time it was pretty universal. Later MESA Boogie amplifiers also pioneered the use of switchable channels, enabling the player to use a footswitch to change from clean to overdrive during a song.

JAHNS AND THE 75 Otherwise, after the disappointing results with solid state, Fender largely tried to keep in touch with the power race which was being won hands down by companies such as Acoustic and Ampeg. Fender's head of engineering at this time was Ed Jahns, a man with a remarkable history in audio design. He had worked for the valve manufacturer Tung-Sol, and had even been involved in the US government committee that decided on the choice of frequency band when FM radio was first introduced. What he was not, however, was a guitarist. He did not have an instinctive understanding of what type of sound was musical. He was, on the other hand, able to call on the assistance of the indefatigable Freddie Tavares, who said in a 1978 interview that "we're designing in greater and greater distortion potential. It's the way of the future."

Ed Jahns' Fender 75 amplifier, of 1979, was an honest attempt to mimic some of the innovations seen in the MESA Boogie II, notably multiple volume

controls and channel switching, which he achieved through silent optical switches rather than MESA's relatively primitive and click-prone relays. In all his amplifiers he achieved extremely high outputs from the same old 6L6 valves.

His principal innovation, borrowed from the so-called "ultra linear" hi-fi amplifier design, was to connect the screen grids of the output valves to the high voltage DC supply via a tap on the amplifier's output transformer. Jahns says that this method gave "lower output impedance and better response over the audio range." It also allowed him to introduce a power switch which could cut the amp's 75W clean output down to 25W and bring in overdrive distortion at a much lower level. "I think that was a wonderful amplifier," says Jahns. "Every part was the best part you could get. It would put out at least 75W from 50Hz to 20kHz at five per cent distortion maximum. It sold like hot cakes." Nonetheless, that particular circuit was not universally admired: some complain of weird distortions caused by ripple currents. It was used on the 75's siblings, the 30 and 140, then dropped. Subsequent Fender amps returned to the traditional output stage design.

TOP SWITCH In 1981, CBS decided it was time for new management at Fender, a response to a sudden drop in sales and profits. The strength of the home market had meant that Fender had always made money for CBS. But by the early 1980s, the overall instrument market in the US had slipped; what sales there were increasingly went to far-eastern companies or far-eastern guitars sold by US manufacturers. So CBS decided to head-hunt several top men from Yamaha's US company. John McLaren became president of CBS's music division, Bill Schultz became president of Fender, Robert Sandell became Fender's head of sales and Dan Smith was hired as head of marketing, electric guitars. All told, about 16 former Yamaha employees joined Fender.

EASTERN PROMISE The new men immediately started a vigorous attempt to revive the ailing company. CBS allowed Fender to retain more than $2m for research and development and new tooling at the Fullerton plant, which by now was making mainly guitars, Rogers drums (that company was acquired in 1968) and Fender Rhodes electric pianos. In addition, Fender started to buy guitars from Japan and elsewhere in the far east. Ironically, given his background, Bill Schultz tried to wrap himself in the flag: he made impromptu speeches to the workforce on the trade battle between America and Japan, hung red, white and blue banners in the factory and used the stars and

Ed Jahns' Fender 75 was the most innovative valve amp in years. A power switch cuts output to 25W for studio use.

CONCERT 112

The name "Concert" has been used on many different amplifiers between the early 1960s and the present day. The 1982 model was available in 1 x 12in, 2 x 10in, 4 x 10in and "top" versions.

With the arrival of a new management team in the early 1980s, serious attempts were made to revive Fender's fortunes in the amplifier market. Designed by Ed Jahns at the behest of Paul Rivera, the Concert was a new valve amplifier that boasted 60W output, two switchable channels and an effects loop with level controls. Nonetheless, it was extremely traditional in appearance

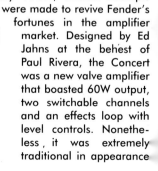

stripes in brochures sent out to the workforce in their pay-packets.

Roger Balmer, who had also been at Yamaha before moving to Music Man, became vice president of marketing and research & development. He looked around for someone to inject new life into the amplifier line and approached a man called Paul Rivera, who had a long and fascinating history as an amplifier designer/guru – and little experience of corporate life.

Like so many others in the Fender amplifier story, including Leo and Don Randall, Rivera had been a ham radio enthusiast. Ham radio is a demanding

hobby that insists upon a knowledge not only of morse code but of electronic theory. Playing guitar and mending friends' amplifiers, and working for a while as an apprentice at Ampeg, Rivera acquired enough expertise to open his own custom amp shop in San Diego, California, building massively powerful Fender copies for bass players and modifying Marshalls. Later he designed solid state amplifiers for Yamaha and even built and sold a few MESA Boogies.

and circuitry. Like the other amplifiers of this late-CBS period, the Concert died when the company was sold to its new owners, who would go on to produce their own range. The Concert is effectively a high-powered version of the 20W Deluxe Reverb II, and is built on the same chassis. But that amplifier has no effects loop circuitry.

he new valve amps introduced by ender in 1982. The Super Champ, particular, is of growing interest to ollectors as well as players.

In January 1981, he was hired by Fender, secretly, before joining officially in May. "They hired me as director of marketing for amplifiers, to get them back into the amp business," he says, "because at that time they had a very small line of basically the same products they'd had since time began. They didn't have any solid state amps [which by now were well established in most manufacturers' ranges] and they didn't have anything that was really competitive in the market.

"They couldn't give the damn things away. Their sales were down to about 10,000 units a year, and for Fender that was like they were out of the amp market. It was expensive valve stuff that didn't even sound modern. Where was our Marshall killer? Where was the amp that the guy could go into a club and cut a date with that had some popular sounds on it?"

Rivera brought with him a five year plan "and everything from front panel designs to a bunch of schematics." He wasn't very impressed with what he

found. "They had a reissue of the Fender Bassman 4 x 10 in R&D development but I felt the time wasn't right to put it out: it was time to push the envelope and get Fender re-established."

He had his own plans for what was needed but first of all he had to tackle what he calls "Corporate BS". "Ed Jahns, the chief engineer, wasn't a guitar player and the marketing guys previous to my coming in couldn't really speak electronics. So there was a huge problem in trying to tell R&D what to do. R&D at that time was an autonomous country club which did not respond well to marketing: marketing were the enemies, and R&D knew where it was at.

"If you look at most of the Fender amp dogs that they came out with, most of them were because there wasn't a really good marketing input. When I got there Ed Jahns was about 72. The problem is he didn't understand what guitar players wanted. Distortion to him was a foreign thing.

"It had only happened because blues players turned up their amps. They had cheap small amps, and it sounded good." White players imitated the sounds they had heard, using fuzz boxes where necessary, or turning up Marshalls and Hiwatts to the point where they would begin to scream. Jahns was persuaded to adapt his design philosophy to meet the new demands of the market, as interpreted by Rivera. "He told me what he wanted," says Jahns, "and I built it just the way he liked it. I always felt, 'Give Sales what they want.'"

Fender's engineers had by this time achieved miracles in terms of getting high output from basically the same valve circuitry they had always used. But there was a penalty. Fender was by now using a 6L6 valve called the STR387, which stood for "Special Tube Replacement". "It was God's gift," says Rivera, "It had superior screen dissipation [meaning it could be run at higher voltages, producing more output] and it had good gain. It should have been given another tube number it was so good."

But there were two problems. Firstly, using a valve at such high voltages does not enhance the quality of the sound. Valves run at lower voltages tend to distort more readily and to produce a more mid-rangey, warmer sound. Secondly, designing an amplifier around the very best valves available does nothing to help those who may have to use inferior quality components in the field. "Pity those poor blokes who are in the middle of Timbuktu who get these Eastern European 6L6s or some other duff tube: instant firecracker!

"To demonstrate my point, I brought in some Eastern European 6L6s, in long skinny bottles with a pinched neck. I put them in the amplifier and, of course, they blew up within a minute or two. I said, 'You have to make these amps run more conservatively. Excuse my language, but fuck the power race.'" In his own valve amps, he held power down for the sake of tone and reliability.

The amps he now introduced were modelled on the customised combos he had produced in the past, incorporating multiple volume controls and channel switching. "One of them, which was one from my childhood, was the Super Champ. The first wacko amp that I ever built was when I was a very young boy, I built a 70W Champ and used it through a 2 x 12in extension cabinet. So when I came on board I thought, marvellous, let's capture all those modified Princeton customers [like the people who'd bought Randall Smith's first MESA Boogies] and let's produce a little Champ that kicks ass."

LESS IS MORE The result was the 18W Super Champ, using a pair of 6V6 output valves driving a 10in speaker. A pull switch on the first volume brings in a "lead" channel that receives a hefty boost by being fed direct

from the reverb driver valve. Perhaps because of its origins in experimentation and modification, the Super Champ brought back some of the sense of fun that characterised the early years of Fender amplification. Uniquely amongst post-CBS Fender amps, it has achieved some appeal for the more open-minded of collectors and players. A simpler version without reverb or the channel switching was issued as the Champ II, and a modified version of the same chassis provided a Bassman 20, with a single 15in speaker. The Princeton Reverb II and Deluxe Reverb II, both delivering 20W into a single 12in speaker, were in the same vein.

True to his word, Rivera also pulled back the Twin Reverb from the power-crazed extremes it had reached. His Twin Reverb II offered channel switching and an effects loop but dropped output to 105W from the 135W it had recently reached. The Super Reverb and Pro Reverb, both recently remodelled into the new blackface look while retaining their silverface era 70W output and circuitry, were allowed to die and replaced by the Concert, a new variant on an old name, which came in 1 x 12in, 2 x 10in and 4 x 10in versions and produced only 60W from the same output valves, in keeping with Rivera's "less is more" philosophy.

The new valve amps were shown at the 1982 NAMM show, but by that time Rivera was well into the second part of his five-year plan, the creation of a credible solid-state range. These amps, which would bear the names London, Montreux and Showman, were designed by Bob Haigler and Bill Hodges. "Bob Haigler had been involved in the solid state designs as early as the Libra/Capricorn period [the Zodiac range]. He was an engineer out of Aerospace Rockwell, but he was brilliant. The problem was he didn't understand distortion or anything like that. When he was directed and had things explained he did brilliant design. The other fellow, Bill Hodges, had the same problem. He was superb in analogue audio – but he didn't understand. So what we did was use the new Fender valve amps that I had helped design and used them as a tone

reference. And we actually came up with several breakthroughs, because those early solid state amps sounded very good. They were workhorses, they were very reliable, lightweight and had some nice features." Externally, no attempt was made this time to separate the solid state amps from the rest of the line. They looked like Fender amps always had. Internally, they showed the evidence of ten years of technological developments. They used "op amps", a new integrated circuit device employing several transistors on a single silicon chip, which permitted more complex circuitry than would have been economical with discreet components. Field Effect Transistors, which in some ways are said

This 1983 ad for the Twin Reverb II emphasises its traditional qualities rather than its innovations.

Only the Strong Survive.
Twin Reverb II: the evolution continues.

Few creations of modern technology have survived long enough to give birth to their own legends. The Fender Twin® amplifier is one of the elite few.

Conceived in the turbulent early years of rock & roll, the Twin grew and flourished with the music it helped to create. Today it is unquestionably the most widely recognized and imitated amplifier in the world.

But the history of the Twin has not been a static one; it has continually evolved with the music it was designed for.

Today's new Twin Reverb II is the most elegant expression yet of this evolution – a modern pinnacle of vacuum tube technology. It retains the explosive power and almost magical warmth of its predecessors, while adding state-of-the-art features like channel switching and an external effects loop with level-controls. And now, for the first time, the Twin is available as a separate top.

Combining the best of the past with the important developments of the present, the Twin Reverb II is an eloquent and charismatic statement of Fender philosophy and Fender art.

You may savor its riches now at any Fender dealer.

THE SOUND THAT CREATES LEGENDS

TWIN REVERB II

The Twin Reverb II introduced such modern features as channel switching and the effects loop to one of the old favourites.

Introduced in 1983, the Twin Reverb II was one of the short-lived products of the Paul Rivera period. Designed by Ed Jahns to Rivera's specifications, it was also made available in a "head" or "top" version.

to mimic the performance of valves, were also employed. Hi-fi type transistor amplifiers have the effect of damping down speaker movements because of the low impedence they present to the speaker. This is considered undesirable in a guitar amplifier, and great ingenuity has been employed by transistor amplifier designers to alter it. The Rivera era transistor amps used special power amp techniques to try and achieve a more valve amp-like interaction between power amplifier stage and loudspeaker.

Rivera's philosophy is one that had by now become common among amplifier designers: "You're talking about the difference between a reproducer and a musical instrument. In my opinion a guitar amp is a musical instrument."

BOARDS & SPEAKERS By now, Fender's problems with manufacturing solid state equipment were long past. In particular, they had mastered the art of building electronic equipment on printed circuit boards, in which the wiring is replaced by conductive metal tracks etched into the boards on which the components are placed. They had a fully-fledged and capable

LONDON REVERB

The London Reverb was a 100W solid state amplifier produced as a "top" and in 1 x 10in and 2 x 12in combo form.

The search for a successful solid state amplifier continued under Paul Rivera. The London Reverb was one of the most powerful and sophisticated attempts, featuring two midrange controls and a five-band graphic equaliser as well as the channel switching that was now a standard feature. The transistor amp continued to gain ground.

The Stage Lead 212 (right) was a 100W transistor combo that eschewed over-complicated controls.

printed circuit production line, having produced boards for a range of pedals and the Rhodes electric piano.

But some bugbears remained. Fender's valve amps had traditionally used what is sometimes called "fish paper" circuit boards. The boards were not printed circuit boards: they merely anchored the components, which were wired together by point to point soldering. By the early 1980s this had become horrendously expensive. There had also been terrible problems in the 1970s with the boards themselves becoming contaminated with moisture and conductive chemicals, making instability a major problem. But attempts to introduce widespread use of printed circuits into the valve amps were rebuffed. The instability was solved by baking the boards and then sealing them with wax: this remained the norm for valve amplifiers, though all the transistor amplifiers were built on printed circuits.

Jensen, the suppliers of Fender's speakers in the 1950s and 1960s, had long since lost interest in the music industry, turning instead to the supply of equipment for car stereos. Most of America's loudspeaker manufacturers had supplied Fender by this time. In Rivera's day, the speaker supplier switched from Pyle to Eminence at the behest of Bill Hughes, who had arrived at Fender from Ampeg, initially to take charge of speaker engineering, though he was also involved in the design of the Concert 112 amplifier.

KNEE-JERK CBS Despite the impetus provided by the new management team, the dead weight of CBS still pressed down on the company. Rivera's account of life under CBS is a mixture of amusement and exasperation. "It was the first time I'd worked for a large corporation. I'd mostly been self-employed during my life. When I came into it first I was in culture shock because I didn't realise that competence wasn't rewarded. It was whose ass were you sucking on, and if you went to a meeting, did you have a bigger stack of papers than the person sitting next to you?" Like many of the people who passed through the CBS-era Fender, he tells of a remote management, prone to knee-jerk decision making and hopelessly in thrall to the theoretical ideas of expensive, hired-in "consultants".

At this time, some veterans remained. Rivera was amazed to find that some of the "girls" on the assembly line had hand-wired prototype amplifiers for Leo himself. And Freddie Tavares hung on just long enough to see out the CBS era. "If anybody could get an express ticket to heaven, this guy was on the bullet train," says Rivera. "He was one of the most magnificent humans. Freddie was a very forgiving person. He'd just laugh it off and say, 'Oh, those guys!' What else could he do? If someone was a most atrocious human being he'd just turn his back and smile and go on to the next subject and ignore it."

MEXICAN BOARDS Part of the problem was CBS's insistence on spreading its vast corporate overheads around the group. Fender had to pay what are called "corporate allocations", almost a kind of internal tax, simply for the pleasure of being part of the giant conglomerate. Production of the amplifiers was moved out of Fullerton, even though Fender had a giant plant there. Amplifier boards were constructed in Mexico, and then transferred to Hoopeston,

Illinois, where Gulbransen Organs had a factory. Fender's amps were then lumbered with the overheads commensurate with organ-building, a slow and labour intensive job when compared to amplifier manufacture. The result was to make it impossible to produce the amplifiers at a competitive price.

FENDER JAPAN The salvation of the company at this stage was a deal that had been struck in 1982, creating Fender Japan. Fender was taking a hammering in the guitar market, with the soaring value of the dollar relative to the yen making Japanese imports, many of them virtual replicas of

Fender's guitars, irresistibly cheap. So negotiations were opened with two Japanese companies, Kanda Shokai and Fender distributor Yamano Music. The joint venture was established with six seats on the board: three for Fender USA, two for Kanda and one for Yamano. Fender USA also owned 38 per cent of the stock of the new company, which was obliged to pay Fender a substantial royalty on any products it sold anywhere in the world. This was soon to prove an extremely valuable source of revenue.

A company called Fuji Gen-Gakki of Matsumoto was hired to produce Squier guitars, which it did at extremely competitive prices. Fender Japan also acquired a factory in the north of Japan, at Utsunomiya, previously employed in making karaoke machines. Fender immediately set it the task of producing a new series of predominantly small transistor amplifiers, the Sidekicks. "They were wonderful people and I had a wonderful relationship with them," says Rivera. "We developed the Sidekick series and in the first year we sold 65,000 pieces in Japan alone.

"There was a small contingent of engineers there. Two engineers actually did the physical work on the engineering. I directed them, I led them, I brought them the circuits but they actually did the physical work. And thank God for that, because it would have been very hard for me as a foreign engineer to design for their system of production."

TAIWAN TOO The Sidekicks became a very extensive range. Further amplifiers were manufactured in Taiwan, under the Squier label, and all these were to become very important in keeping Fender in the amplifier market during the next, post-CBS phase of its history. Currently, though, all the far eastern amplifier imports to the US have been halted, in favour of Mexico.

Paul Rivera claims that in the four years he was with Fender, amplifier sales increased from 10,000 units to 125,000 units a year. "The fact is, I did get them back in the amp market, because I built some cool amps." It must be noted, however, that later observers have been less enthusiastic about the Rivera era product. "Paul Rivera had the right idea with

SQUIER 15

The Squier 15, currently assembled in Mexico, is the last of the foreign-built amplifiers to be imported into the US.

An extensive range of small amplifiers, derived from Fender Japan and made mainly in Japan and Taiwan, was marketed under the Squier and Sidekick labels from 1982 to the present day.

An advertisement for the Sidekicks (below), dating from 1987. They kept the Fender name alive in the amp market.

SWITCHER

The Fender Switcher is a Taiwan-built channel-switching solid state amp typical of the Squier/Sidekick line.

The Switcher (which is also known as the Squier Switcher, and Sidekick or SK Switcher) brought comprehensive channel-switching (A, B or both) to the practice amp market.

This 1983 Sidekick catalogue (above) shows the first models in a range that grew and grew. Especially recommended for roller-skating keyboard players.

switchable amps," says one member of the current Fender team, "but it was like, every sound but the right sound." Of course, every generation of Fender engineers has always believed itself to be in possession of that sound.

The commercial improvements that were made in the early 1980s were not enough to convince CBS of the company's long-term future. Dan Smith, Paul Rivera's opposite number on the guitar side, has an amusing way of describing what happened. "I like to tell people we had four and a half years where we delivered loaves and fishes, and they wanted us to walk on water. We just didn't do the right miracle."

CBS SELL In the third quarter of 1984, CBS's Columbia Group made an operating loss of $8.3m, which it blamed on "continued losses in the musical instruments business". Wall Street analysts estimated that CBS musical instruments alone had lost $2.5m in 1983 and double that in 1984. The revival seemed to be over, even though the new management had taken bold steps to bring the company into the modern world: by 1983, only 20 per cent of the items in the Fender catalogue were more than 18 months old. With its usual acumen, CBS touted Fender around to any guitar company which might be interested. In the meantime, it announced that Fullerton would close in February 1985, with the loss of the remaining 275 jobs on the site. The Illinois amplifier plant had already been turned into a warehouse.

In February 1985, it was revealed that CBS had offered the company to a group of 10 "Fender employees and foreign distributors", led by Bill Schultz

(left). He said that this group would own 51 per cent of the company and the remaining shares would be sold to an unnamed venture capital firm.

POST-CBS Paul Rivera, meanwhile, had attached himself to a rival bid for the company, led by his boss, Roger Balmer, underwritten by the Bass brothers. The bid failed, and, says Rivera, he found himself "persona non grata" with the new regime. "My boss was nuked and so was I," he says, wryly. Suffering what he calls "a mid-life crisis", he went off round the world and came back to found a new, tiny company building initially a rack-mounted valve guitar amp of the kind Fender would never let him put into production because he couldn't promise huge sales. Since then he has expanded into combos, promising aficionados of valves a combination of American and British sounds: notwithstanding a life-long enthusiasm for solid state, he recognises that there is no role for the small manufacturer in that market.

Despite a certain amount of pique about the manner of his departure from Fender, Rivera is not bitter. Of Bill Schultz, he says, "I think he has done a tremendous job and I congratulate him." And he is still grateful for having had the chance to work for what he calls "FU", for Fender University. "Working for Fender was a great experience. I met some of the greatest people I could ever have met, internationally, and I learned a tremendous amount. It was a marvellous experience. Even with all the corporate BS, it was still great."

Fender, meanwhile, was entering another challenging period.

In March 1985, CBS announced that it had sold the battered Fender company to "an investor group led by William Schultz, president of Fender Musical Instruments". The price was $12.5 million: CBS had paid $13m for it in 1965. For his money, Schultz and his investment banking backers acquired the name, the current product lines and whatever inventory was in the warehouses. It did not acquire any buildings, which CBS disposed of separately: the massive Fender factory in Fullerton is now used by a company in the aircraft parts business.

At its CBS peak, Fender's manufacturing division had employed 800 people, with a further 140 at the sales base in Santa Ana. Its annual Fullerton payroll alone was $5 million. The new Fender immediately reduced its workforce to little more than 100 people, took offices in Brea, California, just north east of Fullerton, and began work on establishing itself. The initial concentration was on guitars, imported from Japan while the new company looked for a new base for US production. Amplifiers don't seem to have been a priority. Mike Lewis (left), who is now in charge of amplifier marketing, was then a Fender dealer. "It was all very vague to us. We were actually quite worried about it."

But the dealers wanted amplifiers with the Fender name on them, and for a while the gap was filled by imports from Fender Japan, bearing the Sidekick and Squier names and aimed at the lower end of the market. When the decision was taken to return to amplifier production in the US, Fender looked around for a way of jump-starting the process. In December 1985, they acquired Sunn, an Oregon-based amplification company that had achieved great success in the early 1970s but which had fallen on hard times.

SUNN AND AMPEG
Sunn had been founded in 1963 by brothers Norm and Con Sundholm in a garage behind their family home. In 1965, it moved to Tualatin, a suburb of Portland, Oregon, where they took a lease on a defunct public swimming pool. The man letting it to them filled the pool with dirt and concreted it over: it became their main production area. After achieving great success with high power valve amp designs, Sunn went over to solid state, particularly for its pioneering large-arena PA systems, and faded.

Fender moved its facilities to new premises in Lake Oswego, Oregon. Some of the laid-off Fender R&D people were rehired, and new designers acquired. Under the leadership of Bill Hughes, work began on a new range of Fender amplifiers. Hughes had worked for Ampeg, the other great American amplifier maker. Ampeg's design philosophy had always been very different to Fender's. Their amps had evolved from hi-fi models and boasted ultra-low distortion and massive output power, which made them extremely popular with bass players: Bill Hughes's contribution was an influential 300W monster called the SVT.

MUSIC MAN
Hughes decided that he didn't want to persist with any of the Paul Rivera era products but to make a clean break. He hired, among others, Mark Wentling from Music Man, the company founded by Forrest White and an ex-Fender salesman Tom Walker, who were later joined by Leo Fender after he was released from CBS.

Music Man's amplifiers were amongst the first of the hybrids, mixing solid state and valve technology in the same chassis. Their early versions used op-amps throughout, with the exception of a pair of valves in the output stages. This has the advantage of retaining the type of interaction between circuitry and loudspeaker that is particular to valve amplification. Players tend to feel more of an organic connection with valve amplification: it seems to be more responsive to their own playing dynamics. This characteristic comes from valve power sections (and valve power supplies, though they have all but disappeared).

On the other hand, a valve power section normally amplifies cleanly at normal output levels. The Music Man valves run cool, which improves their longevity but means they do not produce an overdriven sound: the distortion by now considered essential in guitar amplifiers had to be generated earlier on, in the solid state op-amp pre-amplifier section, and, as we have heard, solid state distortion is less inherently acceptable than valve distortion.

TRI-MODE Later hybrids would tend to reverse things, using valves in the pre-amp section to produce the required distortion and then amplifying that sound relatively cleanly through a transistor power amplifier section. As well as making the valve quality of the sound more apparent, this had advantages in terms of weight and cost.

Wentling did not waste much time. His first amplifier for Fender was the Champ 12, announced in autumn 1986. This was a pure valve amplifier (with the exception of a single Field Effect Transistor in the reverb circuit) putting out 12W from three valves. The push-pull output stage of the Super Champ was eschewed in favour of the single output valve that had been traditional in previous Champs.

Two more amps were put in train at the same time and made their debut in 1987. The Dual Showman, in what used to be called piggy-back style (now normally referred to as a "head" or "top" and a "cab"), shared a chassis with The Twin, a radical reinterpretation of Fender's long-standing flagship. Common to both was something called "Tri-Mode", which allowed the two channels to be used independently with two separate instruments, in foot-switchable mode, or simultaneously so that both channels' sounds could be mixed. Both used four 6L6s to provide 100W, but in recognition of the modern vogue for playing at lower volumes and putting the sound into a PA system a switch was provided to cut output to 25W. The Showman made do without reverb but included a three-way damping switch to alter the way its power stage and speaker interacted.

SIGNED AMP One of Hughes's innovations was to increase the identification between an individual designer and the amplifier he was working on. "At Fender, a project is assigned to an engineer. He works with the marketing person, Mike Lewis, and the amplifier circuitry is designed, massaged, gotten into shape. The same engineer lays out the circuit boards, designs the speaker cabinets and designs all the documentation and assembly aids for the factory. The designer actually writes the owner's manual. That's the only way to do it. One person has to walk it through: I don't like committees. We don't even have printed circuit layout people here. The boards are laid out and designed by the project engineer. His signature is in the corner of the drawing. His initials are on the PC board. He is ultimately responsible."

SOLID APPROVAL By now it was apparent that solid state amplifiers had achieved an important place in the market, simply on account of their practicality. Overall, many more solid state amps were being sold than valve amps, and Fender needed to enter that market. Hughes had been on hand for the Rivera era solid state amps and now he was prepared for another attempt at cracking a market that had never been happy for Fender.

"The only thing that has happened with semi-conductors over the last 30 years is that they have got quieter and more reliable," he says. "The circuit design techniques that we are using currently are the same techniques that

PRO 185

The first amplifiers of the post-CBS Fender company attempted to cater for all tastes, offering low-power valve sounds, high-power solid state amplification and even a chorus effect.

Once the new owners of the Fender company had taken the decision to produce amplifiers and found new premises in Oregon, design work moved on apace. The first amplifier was the Champ 12 (left), a new valve amp bearing a famous name and producing just 12W from a single 6L6 output valve. At one stage it was available to special order in snakeskin, a mark of the new Fender's willingness to could have been used in 1965. It's just a matter of learning what to do. The big difference is that the people who design solid state amplifiers now understand how tube amplifiers work. Solid state amplifier designers back in 1965 didn't pay attention to how tubes work. Every one of my amp engineers who designs solid state has also designed tube amps."

FAST FOUR Work started on the first solid state range early in the life of the new Fender company, to be designed by Mark Wentling and Bill Hughes. The range came to be known as the Fast Four: the 85, the Deluxe 85, the Stage 185 and the Pro 185. Effectively these were all the same amplifiers, using uprated power circuitry in the latter pair, and with the Pro 185 using a pair of 12in Eminence speakers rather than the single 12in driver that was used in the rest. They all boasted highly complex tone circuitry and controls with such labels as "contour" and "tilt". According to Lewis, "This was actually the first successful implementation of solid state electronics in Fender's history. They were the first amps that sounded good, were priced well and were successful."

embrace fleeting fashions. More significant was the 160W Pro 185, one of the so-called Fast Four, a series of solid state amplifiers combining complex tone circuitry with a valiant stab at a traditional Fender sound. Although welcomed by product-starved dealers, their red-knob, black grille cosmetics were unpopular. Later the Pro 185 was remodelled as one of the "Standard Series", using a very traditional blackface look. By this stage, features were becoming more important than sheer power, the majority of amplifiers being used in home or studio. The Princeton Chorus (right) was one of a brace of US-built amplifiers using a stereo chorus effect.

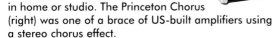

Fender didn't make it easy for itself, initially. The company's marketing department felt that the traditional new blackface Fender look, with silver grille cloth and black knobs, was now inextricably associated with the products of the previous Fender ownership. It decided that the time was right for a radical change of appearance, to announce to the world that here was a new company with new products.

Mike Lewis attended the launch of the new line, in 1988, as a dealer. "It was a bitter-sweet thing. It was like, 'Oh boy, they've finally got a bunch of new American-made amps. Oh, they've got red knobs on 'em!'"

The look was followed across the whole of the line as it existed then. The cabinets were traditional in shape and finish. The front panels looked broadly

similar to the usual blackface, except for the sheer density of print demanded by the complex new tone controls. The grille cloth, however, was plain black. And, most disturbingly, the knobs were deep, narrow, and scarlet. Traditionalists were unimpressed but despite that dealers gritted their teeth and ordered the new product. Later, there would be a rethink.

For now, it was a case of adding more amplifiers to the line. Two US-built solid state stereo chorus amplifiers were introduced, the first time Fender had used the effect, in which a single instrument is played through two built-in amplifiers with a variable time delay between them. This was about as far away from the no-frills world of the tweed Champs and Princetons as it is possible to imagine. A third, the 2 x 10W SK Chorus 20, was a Sidekick model imported from Japan where such advanced signal processing had long been the norm.

Another set of valve amps arrived very shortly, starting with the Super 60 in early 1989. Variants, the Super 112 and the Super 210, followed some time later, the difference between them being in speaker complement and controls. Some idea of the differential established by now between solid state and valve amplifiers can be gained by comparing the list price of the Super 60 in 1990, $669.99, and that of its transistor opposite number, the 85: $399.99. Valve amplification was rapidly pricing itself out of the mass market. Even the entry level Champ 12 had edged up to $339.99 by 1990, a startling price for a 12W amplifier. A 15W Sidekick Japanese-made transistor combo cost $159.99.

The Super 60 also benefited from the red-knob treatment, which had the unfortunate effect of making an expensive valve amp look indistinguishable from a budget solid state model. It would become apparent that musicians, especially aspiring players, are no more immune to snobbery than anyone else.

But those who had been driven into apoplexy by the red knob models had some more shocks in store. First Fender made the Champ 12 available in a variety of "special" coverings that included red, white, grey and a particularly grotesque snakeskin. Then, at the end of 1989, it announced the M80.

The M80 looked and sounded like nothing in Fender's history. Aimed squarely at young heavy-metal enthusiasts, the original 90W combo came wrapped in what the catalogue blithely described as grey "carpet", with plastic

M-80

Fender's M-80 was an unashamed bid to capture the affections of young players wanting masses of accessible distortion.

The M-80 combo of 1990 was a radical departure in both sound and appearance. Red knobs and grey "carpet" covering were coupled with transistor circuitry producing an instantly raucous sound. It was marketed as Fender's HM amp, with great success. The version pictured was the product of a mid-1990s rethink that gave the amp a more traditional look.

J.A.M.

Part of the M-80 family, the J.A.M. amp was aimed at young guitarists in a hurry.

The J.A.M. combo of 1990 is a very long way from the Fender amps of yesteryear. Tone and overdrive control are by means of switches, which makes for instant gratification rather than subtlety. Its chorus effect is unusual in a budget amplifier. It has an aggressive appearance.

The J.A.M. offers little comfort for traditionalists, even in later less flamboyant versions.

corners. It was unashamedly a solid-state amp promising, in addition to an attempt at a traditional Fender sound, "the most radical distortion of any amplifier on the market". The original M80 spawned head and chorus versions, and then a low-powered trio, R.A.D, H.O.T. and J.A.M., in which traditional rotary controls were complemented by push-buttons giving instant access to pre-programmed levels of distortion. These were not amplifiers for the purist, who traditionally expected to learn to master his amplifier as he had done his instrument, but for young players in search of instant gratification. They have been a tremendous success.

Mike Lewis explains: "I don't suppose they thought that only beginners were going to use them, but that's the way it turned out. It took us into a whole new market. Younger players then didn't have much awareness of Fender heritage – they just wanted a sound.

'63 VIBROVERB

Meticulous modern recreation of a short-lived amplifier of the early 1960s. The only brown Tolex amp in the series.

Fender's Vibroverb reissue is based on the first version, the 6G16 model, which uses two 10in speakers. Purists prefer this version to the later model with a single 15in speaker because of certain peculiarities of the circuitry. In particular, its tremolo circuit (called vibrato in this instance) operates by modulating the biasing of the power valves. Later models simply earth the signal at the vibrato frequency. Their reverberation and tone control circuits are also slightly different.

'65 TWIN REVERB

The modern recreation of one of the classics of the immediate pre-CBS era, the 1965 blackface Twin Reverb achieves a very high level of visual accuracy.

When the new Fender company established in 1985 was looking for an early model to produce in a reissue version, the blackface Twin Reverb of 1965 was a natural choice. It has always had a great reputation as an amp for the working musician, being powerful, robust and portable, and as such is still widely used.

"The largest number of buyers for guitars and amplifiers, originally, back in the 1950s, were actual working players. There weren't as many beginners and garage bands and stuff. When the 1960s came, with the Beatles, everybody bought guitars like they were clothing.

"Now we have a lot of people who just play in their bedrooms and they want to get that big Marshall amp cranked-up sound at transistor radio volume at two o'clock in the morning. And you can't do that with an old Champ amp; you can't do that with a tweed Deluxe. Those amps were never meant for that, they were meant to be played in a real musical situation. Whereas nowadays the largest selling models are designed to sound good in your bedroom."

REISSUE TIME The M80 and its progeny certainly fitted the bill. But Fender had, and has, ambitions at the other end of the market. In 1990, it launched a reissue of the 1959 Bassman, a version of which Paul Rivera had vetoed when he arrived at Fender while it was still owned by CBS in the early

'65 DELUXE REVERB

This reissue of one of the most desirable of small guitar amps even uses a replica of the original Jensen speaker.

The original blackface Deluxe is compact and portable and produces rich overdrive distortion at comparatively low levels. The reissue attempts to offer a very similar package to modern players.

'59 BASSMAN

The most acclaimed of all the reissue models, the '59 Bassman reintroduced tweed to the Fender range after 30 years.

The original "four-hole" 4 x 10in Bassman of 1959 is probably the most sought after of all vintage amplifiers. The reissue goes a long way towards the appearance and sound of the originals.

The introduction of the '59 Bassman made tweed fashionable once again. Fender has since produced a whole tweed range.

1980s. This time round, the timing was right. According to Mike Lewis: "As soon as we did it, that was the beginning of when the professionals and the artists started using brand new Fender amplifiers again. All of a sudden Eric Clapton was playing a Bassman. The old amps were getting hard to find, expensive and hard to maintain – and here we were making them again."

The process of producing the reissue models, which now also include a 1963 Vibroverb in brown tolex, a 1965 Twin Reverb in black and a 1965 Deluxe Reverb, is not as uncomplicated as it might seem. It starts with the original documentation which was acquired with the company. Then the country is scoured for good examples of the amplifier in question to use as a model. As always with Fender, all sorts of people, inside and out, are asked to make an evaluation before the best version is picked and closely replicated.

Closely, but not slavishly, you might say. "We don't have to use modern components," says Lewis, "but we do. If we were going to build them exactly the way they used to, with the old fish paper and eyelets and hand wiring and point to point soldering, a '59 Bassman would retail for $3,000." In fact, it currently goes for $1,129.99, which undercuts the bespoke vintage amp makers, such as Kendrick or THD. Of course, the Fender reissues are still mass-produced amplifiers, whereas the $1,899 Kendrick 4 x 10in Bassman replica is hand-wired at a rate of no more than two a week.

Fender uses printed circuit boards, which enrages a tiny number of purists, but otherwise things are pretty close to the originals. The cabinets and chassis are the same, as are the Tolex, tweed and fittings. The same component suppliers are sought out where possible, but the disappearance of Jensen from the instrument speaker market means Fender has had to commission replicas of the old Concert Series 12in drivers. The Oxford company, one of Leo Fender's original suppliers, still provides the two 10in speakers in the Vibroverb.

In 1991, Fender's administrative headquarters moved from Brea to Scottsdale, Arizona. Mike Lewis, who had by now joined the company in sales, became marketing manager for amplifiers, with a brief to re-establish the

company as America's number one amplifier vendor. He was immediately sent off around the world to talk to Fender's agents and customers. "We didn't want to do something that was just going to be appropriate to the US. We wanted to do just one set of products that would fit the needs of everybody and that everybody would accept. So we came back and put together a three to five year plan, what we would phase in, what we would phase out, how we would market it and advertise it."

The immediate upshot was the removal of the grey carpet covering from the M80 series. It became black. And the red knobs and black grille cloths featured on the rest of the range were replaced by the traditional black knobs and silver grille cloth. "The main reason was because when you went somewhere to hear a live band and there was a guy playing guitar, eight times out of ten it was going to be a Fender amp. And they never had red knobs.

"So what would happen is that our young wannabe guitar player would go to the club, see this great guitar player, love the sound he's getting, notice he's playing a Fender guitar and take a look at the amp. And there would be this amp with the big red jewel [panel light] on it, and the silver grille cloth, and the Fender silver name plate, and he'd get this warm feeling. And he'd go to the

music store the next day and see the Fender amps in there and none of them would look like that. So there was a broken connection.

"On the other hand, if he saw somebody playing a Peavey or a Marshall and he got turned on by it he could go to the music store and see things exactly like it." So the decision was taken to produce lines of amplifiers that had essentially the same look and philosophy across the range of prices and power outputs. The solid state "Fast Four" were remodelled and renamed to form the basis of the new "Standard Series", which extends from the 15W Bullet up to the 160W Pro 185 and includes the two US-built chorus amps. All have been remodelled into a uniform style, based around a traditional blackface look but with modern faceplates and knobs without numbering, and some of the complexities of the tone control system were removed in the interests of simplicity and economy.

The Super 60 and its derivatives were quietly dropped. "They didn't really sound like an old Fender amp," says Lewis. "The clean channel was a little bit weaker than you'd expect. The overdrive was maybe a little hotter than you'd expect. There wasn't a whole lot of middle ground. When people think of a Fender amp they think of that middle ground, where it crunches when you attack it: turn it up to a certain volume and you play it by your attack. Those amps didn't do it." The Twin and Dual Showman head survived, however, from the first generation of post-CBS amplifiers.

Two new valve amplifiers, the Super and the Concert, were developed with the explicit aim of combining a vintage sound with the facilities deemed essential by modern players, including a line-level output and a front-mounted mix control for returning effects into the final sound. Neither amp has channel switching, that being deemed inconsistent with the vintage ethos.

PRE OR POWER? In keeping with Fender's apparent desire to offer something for everyone, two separate, and quite antithetical, hybrid ranges were offered. The earlier Champ 25 and Champ 25SE produced 25W into a 12in speaker from a circuit that was entirely solid state except for a pair of 6L6s in the output stage. They have been dropped. Lewis: "The reason they put the tubes in the power section was that they asked people what it was about tubes that they liked. And everything that everybody liked about tube amps was produced by the tube power amp, not by the pre-amp." Another advantage was that it is easier to make solid state electronics emulate a valve pre-amp than a valve power amp, not to say much cheaper. A valve pre-amp can easily contain five expensive valves. But by the time it was on the market, opinion had swung round to the belief that hybrids ought to have valves in the front end.

Even so, it was apparently a success, which raises the question of why it was dropped. Bill Hughes, who is laconic at the best of times, becomes even more tight-lipped about this. "That was an earlier approach that we walked away from. I am of the opinion that what we are doing now is a lot more logical." Others, outside Fender, suggest the amp had a reliability problem.

EMOTIONAL VALVES The Performer series is Fender's second attempt at a hybrid, although the use of valve technology is so tokenistic as to

be barely worthy of that description. A single 12AX7 valve sits in the pre-amp and imparts valve colourations to the amp's overdrive performance. Cynics maintain that it is there for purely marketing reasons. Bill Hughes recognises the emotional appeal of valve technology to the guitarist: "Guitar players are used to vacuum tubes. Vacuum tubes impart characteristics to the sound: be they right or wrong, they are what the guitar player is used to."

Certainly these amplifiers, which have been given a slightly modernised blackface look with a red LED instead of a true jewel panel light, sell at high

PERFORMER 1000

The Performer series represents Fender's second stab at "hybrid" amplifier design. Their conservative looks belie their extremely aggressive sound quality.

In the Performer series, which consists of two combos and a head amp and cabinets, Fender has used a single 12AX7 valve in the pre-amp to give a particular colouration to the sound. Interestingly, the valve is connected as a rectifier and plays no part in amplifying the sound.

The Ultra Chorus (left) is a 2 x 65W solid state stereo chorus amplifier that derives from the Power Chorus of 1989.

prices. The 70W Performer 650 is nearly twice the price of the 65W Deluxe 112, its pure solid-state equivalent. It does not, however, sound like a traditional valve amp. "It is a much more aggressive sounding amplifier than you'd expect from Fender," says Lewis.

Lovers of the tweed look are catered for in yet another series, including the Blues Deluxe and Blues De Ville, which are modern valve amps (except the solid state Bronco, which has inexplicably acquired a tweed coat) based on no particular models but clearly in the vintage spirit.

With this plethora of models for guitarists, there's a sense in which the new Fender has neglected bass players. Certainly that's where much attention is going to be directed in future. Hughes has an unparalleled record in bass amplification that currently expresses itself only in the BXR series of solid state heads, combo amps and speaker systems, introduced in 1987.

"Bass players historically feel like everybody thinks they're stupid," says Lewis, "like they're not real musicians. So bass players have developed a bit of

BLUES DE VILLE

A determined attempt to combine the look and feel of a vintage tweed amp with modern valve circuitry and construction. For those with traditional tastes.

Some 40 years after it was first introduced, Fender's diagonal luggage linen, the famous "tweed", is still practical and visually appealing. The Blues De Ville is not a vintage amp, however. It employs modern circuitry and manufacturing techniques in a contemporary reinterpretation of the classic valve combo package, with a tonal bias towards those players still content to work in the blues and rock 'n' roll tradition. It is available with two 12in or four 10in speakers.

The Pro Junior (above) is Fender's smallest and cheapest valve amp.

VIBRO-KING

A dead ringer for an early Tolex amp, the Vibro-King is actually a brand new amp, hand-built at Fender's Custom Shop.

The Custom Shop was established at Fender's headquarters in Scottsdale, Arizona. Its first product, the Vibro-King, combines vintage-style circuitry and looks with modern features.

The Vibro-King's "retro" look is more than just skin-deep. With the rear panel removed, you can see the way it combines a traditional chassis with modern features, such as an effects send and return.

TONE-MASTER

The Tone-Master, an elegant reinterpretation of the Tolex piggy-back look, stands at the pinnacle of Fender's current instrument amplifier range.

The Tone-Master, like the other Custom Shop models, is aimed at the most affluent of customers. Designed by Bruce Zinky, it uses classic 12AX7 and 6L6 circuitry and is hand assembled on a special low-volume line.

The Tone-Master comes with a choice of speaker enclosures, using either two or four 12in Celestion drivers.

a complex about that and they tend to try harder. They actually read the instruction manuals for their amplifiers, and they study all the specs for equipment and make very calculating decisions about what they want to buy. They are much more informed and they are not hung up on tradition." Certainly, bass players were early to embrace solid state amplification, and to this day there is no market among bass players for reissue or vintage products. "They want the latest, greatest thing," says Lewis.

Meanwhile, for guitarists, "the latest, greatest thing" is Fender's amplifier Custom Shop. The guitar Custom Shop, at Fender's instrument plant in Corona, California, has been building limited edition and one-off instruments since 1987. The amplifier Custom Shop, at Scottsdale, was established in 1993 under the direction of Bruce Zinky, who had worked for Matchless, a tiny amplifier company producing hand-made variants on old Vox designs. The idea was to produce amplifiers for players at the top of their profession: put bluntly, it seems to have stemmed from the question, "What have we got that we can offer Eric Clapton?" to which the answer was, "Not much beyond the reissues." But, unlike its guitar equivalent, it is not equipped to produce one-off models. Rather it hand-builds its own limited range, using the best components in vintage-style circuitry with modern facilities, at the rate of about nine amplifiers a week. Its first models, the Vibro-King 3 x 10in 60W combo and the Tone-Master piggy-back amplifier, were widely acclaimed, although their prices are extraordinary. The Vibro-King is Fender's most expensive model, costing $2,499.99 on introduction.

INTO THE 1990s Bill Carson, who joined the Fender payroll in 1957 and is still working part-time for the company, has Vibro-King #1 in his office. He sees it as the best example yet of the revival of Fender, which he says is now the strongest he has seen it in 30 years. "For many years there was never the love affair with electronics that there was with the guitar player and his particular instrument," he says. "But the last several years have seen a change." Having stared into the abyss at the time of CBS's exit, Fender has returned to become much stronger than ever, with worldwide sales now many times higher than those achieved then. Carson laughs about the Vibro-King's "corny" name. "That's something Leo or Randall would have thought up in 1949," he says.

Sadly, several of the men who built the Fender amplifier business into what it is today are not around to see the Vibro-King, although they would surely have approved. Doc Kauffman, whose casual visit to Leo Fender's radio shop set the whole thing in motion, died in June 1990. Freddie Tavares, who brought incalculable musical and engineering expertise to the Fender organisation over 30 years, died a month later. Leo himself was already suffering the effects of Parkinson's disease by that time, though it did not prevent him spending a couple of hours each day in his laboratory at G & L, which he finally owned outright, having bought out George Fullerton in the mid 1980s. The day before he died, on Thursday March 21, 1991, Leo had been at his workbench as usual, tinkering to the last.

REFERENCE
SECTION

USING THE REFERENCE SECTION

The reference section that follows comprises a comprehensive list of Fender amplifiers, from the K&F produced by Doc Kauffman and Leo Fender at the end of World War II to the current products of Fender's factory in Oregon. Amplifier names appear in alphabetical order: variant types (for instance, the TV front, wide panel and narrow panel versions) appear in chronological order beneath the main heading provided by the amplifier's name. Modern variants with similar names appear after the classic versions.

The reference listings use a simple condensed format to convey a great deal of information. In each case, the main description is based on the amplifier as it was on its introduction. Minor variations from that are listed in italic type. Major variations, provided they are not solely cosmetic, get a new listing of their own.

It is difficult to overestimate the number of variants that exist during the years when Fender was making its most significant amplifiers. It is worth remembering that production runs were relatively small and that there was a process of almost constant change in specifications and appearance. Some of these changes were deliberate, others less so. Forrest White has talked of the chaos in inventory and stock control when he arrived as plant manager in 1954. It is not unknown for amplifiers to have quite different speakers, valves and control layouts to others of the same type apparently made at about the same time. For all these reasons, therefore, the listings cannot be definitive. An amp may still be genuine even if it does not tally with its listing.

These are the main points covered in the listings:

NAME This is the name by which the amplifier is listed in Fender's documentation. Some amplifiers have acquired different names at different times: these variations should be cross-referenced. Following the name, in italic type, is a broad description of the amplifier's 'family': narrow panel Bassman, brownface Vibroverb etc. I have also used it to differentiate between new and old amplifiers with the same names: for instance the Super Amp of the late 1940s and the current model.

DATE All dates are approximate: this is particularly true of pre-1953 models for which no reliable dating method exists. I have included an approximate start and finish date for each model, but it is worth noting that no such sharp cut-off actually took place. Many models stayed in stock long after they had ceased production. Models which are still in production have just a date of introduction. Models which came and went within a year have only that year.

CABINET I have broken the many types of cabinet down into 10 basic types, and they are illustrated on the endpapers inside the front or back cover of this book. **A** is the solid wood, uncovered cabinet used for the earliest models. **B** is the TV-front model, so called because of the shape of the loudspeaker aperture. **C** is the tweed model with deep panels at top and bottom of the speaker aperture and the aperture itself running the full width of the cabinet: this is called the wide panel or broad panel version by collectors. **D** is the "narrow panel" version, in which the speaker aperture extends almost to the edge of the cabinet at top and bottom and on both sides. **E** is the normal combo shape introduced in the early 1960s and which has been the standard shape ever since: I have included bass combos under this general heading. All have a sloping front at the top of the cabinet. **F** is the traditional "piggy-back" shape, introduced in the early 1960s. It means a Tolex-covered box containing the amplifier and a matching loudspeaker cabinet. Obviously many different variants on this pattern are available. **G** is the combo shape used for the first solid state amplifiers only. It has a much deeper and taller slope at the top of the front. **H** means "head" or "top" and "cab": obviously there is an overlap with "piggy-back" but I have used it to identify amplifiers in which the amp box does not conform to the traditional Tolex-covered, silver grille style. **I** is used for amplifiers designed to be mounted in a rack system. **J** is used for the combos and head amps introduced in the late 1980s, in which the wooden box does not slope back at the top.

NAMEPLATE The name Fender appears in many different ways. Early models have no nameplate as such: the name is simply painted on the rear control panel when it appears at all. This method is used at various times over the years. The other variants are again pictured on the endpapers inside the front or back cover. Note that the nameplate is not a reliable method of dating an amplifier: Fender was notorious for using whatever type of nameplate happened to be at hand.

COVERINGS The first Fender amplifiers were simply made of varnished wood. Subsequent models used various types of luggage linen or tweed, some types of which have a "vertical" weave rather than the diagonal version used later. These versions, which I have characterised as "early tweed", come in a variety of different colours, some of which have only arisen due to the effects of time and exposure to sunlight. The classic tweed is off-white with a brown stripe running from 11 o'clock to 5 o'clock irrespective of which way you look at the amp. I have called that "diagonal tweed". It becomes universal with the introduction of the wide-panel cabinet. The Champion 600 sometimes appears in a brown and cream two-tone arrangement in a sort of early vinyl or Naugahyde fabric.

Tolex, which arrives in 1960, is a cloth-backed vinyl type covering. It comes initially in various shades of cream (known as blonde) and brown (known as tan or chocolate) and in various finishes, some smoother than others. I have simplified this very complex area into "cream" or "brown" for reasons of sanity. The cream version was used for the top of the range models. The brown version was applied to the rest. All models went over to black from about 1964/5. The use of a black Tolex-type covering remained universal until the late 1980s when Fender experimented with vivid coloured vinyls (including snakeskin), grey and black "carpet" coverings, and a reintroduced tweed.

GRILLE Early amplifiers used a simple felt or velvet-type cloth in various colours. Later a dark brown was used, although these have faded badly to a reddish hue. True grille cloth was introduced with the wide panel cabinet, usually in a light brown. The first brown Tolex amps continued to use this cloth for a while before acquiring a light brown cloth of their own. White Tolex amps used various maroon and dark brown grille cloths. Silver became universal from the time of the black Tolex finish. It acquired a distinctive blue sheen in the silverface era. Some mid-1980s models used a grey grille cloth.

CONTROL PANEL Leo Fender's first amplifiers, the K&F, have no control panel, and sometimes just a volume control on the back of the cabinet. The Model 26 type Deluxe and Professional have a black painted panel at the back of the cabinet, with volume and tone controls with numbers on the panel. The Champion series followed this general pattern.

Later the chassis of the amplifiers was rejigged so that the control panel was at the rear top of the cabinet, facing up. Again, the numbers are printed on the panel so that a simple pointer type knob can be used. This version is used on TV front, wide panel and narrow panel tweed amplifiers.

The Tolex amplifiers use a forward facing panel. Brownface panels are a dark brown with numbers on them. Blackface panels have no numbers. All have the model name in script. The silverface panel is quite different. It is an aluminium panel, still with no numbers but the model name is in turquoise block capitals. After that there was a reversion to "new blackface", which is similar to the early version but with various minor typographical modifications. All blackface and new blackface amps use knobs with numbers. Other amps use black control panels but with numbers on them: this makes a great deal of difference to the aesthetics. The first generation of solid state amps use an aluminium front panel of quite different design. Post-CBS amps introduced a whole range of different panel treatments.

KNOBS AND CONTROLS The early Fender amps used a standard pointer knob of the kind used on much radio equipment at the time and indeed originated from radio parts suppliers. Some used round knobs with a pointer line. The pointer knobs were universal throughout the tweed era.

Brownface amps in brown Tolex use a flat brown knob with a pointer line inscribed on it. Cream Tolex amps tend to use an off-white knob with a black pointer line. Blackface, silverface and new blackface amps use the classic knob with a raised silver top and numbers around the perimeter. Some new blackface amps use black numbered knobs. Unnumbered knobs in black or red are used with numbered control panels in the post-CBS period. The aluminium solid state control panels have their own rather over-sized aluminium knobs. The second solid state series (the Zodiac amps) use a knob with a black centre and numbers on the edges: after the failure of this series the knobs were distributed to other models.

Controls are listed wherever possible in the order they appear reading left to right. Some abbreviations are used: (v = volume, t = treble, m = mid-range, b = bass, r = reverb, s = tremolo speed, i = tremolo intensity, bs = bright switch, ds = deep switch). Where two or more channels are used, the channel name is followed by the controls for that channel. Controls that apply to both channels come after 'Both:'. Note that tremolo and vibrato are the same thing: a rhythmic fluctuation in volume.

SPEAKERS In the golden years most of Fender's speakers were made by Jensen, although a variety of other makes were used. Later Jensen abandoned the musical instrument market and Fender bought its speakers from other companies. Where the speaker manufacturer is specified (for instance where JBL or Electro-voice speakers are used as a feature) this information is included. Piggy-back amplifiers usually have a choice of different speaker cabinets.

VALVES Early Fender amps used the standard-sized valves then available: these often come in metal tubes and are called 6N7, 6C7, 6SJ7 and similar. Output valves were early versions of the 6V6 and 6L6 valves. Rectifiers use valves whose numbers begin with 5, for instance the 5Y3. In the early 1950s the pre-amp valves were changed to sub-miniature glass types, with the numbers 12AX7 and 12AT7. These permitted more complex circuitry, for instance tremolo and reverb. Later the 12AX7 was sometimes replaced by the 7025 and the 6L6 by the 5881. These are supposed to be exact replacements and should make no difference to the sound. Later valve rectifiers were replaced by solid-state rectifiers, to the dismay of some valve purists. For more information on valve performance and interaction I recommend Gerald Weber's *Hip Vintage Guitar Amps*.

OUTPUT This is listed in watts RMS where that figure is available. It should be noted that there are no accurate figures for the power output of the early amplifiers, all of which are much less powerful than would have been normal later. There is no direct correlation between RMS output figures and actual volume: that depends on loudspeaker efficiency. But low power tube amplifiers will distort at lower volumes than high power amplifiers.

VARIANTS An italic line lists changes of specification where these do not sufficiently alter the character of an amplifier to merit a whole new entry. Contrary to received opinion, some silverface amplifiers are very similar to their blackface forebears except in looks. A further italic line lists points of interest.

DATING FENDER AMPS

Various systems have been proposed for dating Fender amplifiers. None is foolproof and you are always advised to keep your wits about you.

DATE CODE ON TUBE CHART After 1953, Fender amps have a date code stamped on the 'tube chart', inside the speaker compartment on a side panel. It consists of two letters only. The first is the year, starting with A for 1951 and running through to O in 1965. The second is the month: A is January and L is December. Of course, sometimes the date only applies to the tube chart, not the amp.

DATE CODES ON SPEAKERS A six-digit code on the speaker frame indicates the manufacturer and date of the speaker (though not when the amp was made). Jensen's code number is 220. Oxford's is 465. The remaining three digits stand for the year of manufacture and the week in that year. Hence 465317 indicates an Oxford speaker manufactured in the 17th week of 1953 and 220526 indicates a Jensen speaker from the 26th week of 1955. Obviously there is no way of telling the difference between 1953 and 1963, except common sense.

POTENTIOMETER CODES American made potentiometers (volume and tone controls) have a 6 or 7 digit code identifying their manufacturer and date. The first three digits are the maker. The fourth, or fourth and fifth digits, identify the year: 6 could be 1956 or 1966. If it says 66 that is obviously less ambiguous. The final two digits are the week: 22 is the 22nd week. So, 137826 indicates a potentiometer made in the 26th week of 1948, 1958 or 1968. 1066219 indicates a potentiometer made in the 19th week of 1962. For more details on this see Aspen Pittman's *The Tube Amp Book*.

B300

1979-1982
CABINET: STYLE I
NAMEPLATE: NONE

■ Black control panel (numbered); 10 black knobs (v, b, low mid, mid, t, effects, 3-way eq, compressor).
■ Bass amp: no speaker included.
■ Solid state.
■ Output: 300W.
Fender name is painted on front panel.

BANDMASTER *TV front*

1952
CABINET: STYLE B
NAMEPLATE: STYLE 1

■ Early tweed covering; cloth grille.
■ Top control panel (numbered); Two pointer knobs (v, t).
■ Speaker: 1 x 15in Jensen.
■ Valves: 2 x 6SJ7, 6SN7 or 6SL7, 2 x 6L6.
■ Output: c15W.
Some doubts about the existence of this amp. If it does exist it will be virtually identical to Bassman of similar vintage.

BANDMASTER *Wide panel*

1952-1954
CABINET: STYLE C
NAMEPLATE: STYLE 1

■ Diagonal tweed covering; cloth grille.
■ Top control panel (numbered); Two pointer knobs (v, t).
■ Speaker: 1 x 15in Jensen.
■ Valves: 2 x 6SJ7, 6SN7 or 6SL7, 2 x 6L6.
■ Output: c15W.
Extremely rare amp.

BANDMASTER *Narrow panel*

1954-1960
CABINET: STYLE D
NAMEPLATE: STYLE 3

■ Diagonal tweed covering; brown tweed-era grille.
■ Top control panel (numbered); Five pointer knobs (Mic v, Inst v, b, t, p).
■ Speakers: 3 x 10in Jensen.
■ Valves: 12AY7, 12AX7, 2 x 6L6G, 5U4G.
■ Output: c15W.

BANDMASTER *Tolex*

1960-1961
CABINET: STYLE E
NAMEPLATE: STYLE 6

■ Brown Tolex covering; brown tweed-era grille.
■ Brownface control panel (numbered); Nine brown knobs (Normal: b, t, v. Vibrato: b, t, v, s, i. Both: p).
■ Speakers: 3 x 10in Jensen.
■ Valves: 5 x 7025, 2 x 6L6GC, silicon rectifier.
■ Output: 30W.
1960 version has controls in reverse order: bass, treble, volume. Virtually identical chassis to Concert, Pro and Vibrasonic.

BANDMASTER *Piggy-back* (brownface/blackface)

1961-1969
CABINET: STYLE F
NAMEPLATE: STYLE 6

■ Cream Tolex covering; maroon grille.
■ Brownface control panel (numbered); Nine brown knobs (Normal: v, b, t. Vibrato: v, b, t, s, i. Both: p).
■ Speakers: 1 x 12in cabinet.
■ Valves: 4 x 7025, 2 x 12AX7, 2 x 5881, silicon rectifiers.
■ Output: 40W.
From late 1962, 2 x 12in cabinet introduced. From 1963/64, standard blackface control panel and knobs, though not necessarily

black Tolex. Presence control replaced by bright switch. 6L6GC output valves reintroduced.

BANDMASTER *Silverface*

1969-1974
CABINET: STYLE F
NAMEPLATE: STYLE 7

■ Black Tolex covering; silver grille.
■ Silverface control panel; Eight silver-top numbered knobs (Normal: v, b, t. Vibrato: v, b, t, s, i).
■ Speakers: 2 x 12in cabinet.
■ Valves: 2 x 7025, 12AX7, 12AT7, 2 x 6L6GC, silicon rectifiers.
■ Output: 40W.
Output increased to 45W from 1970. Discontinued 1974.

BANDMASTER REVERB *Piggy-back*

1970-1981
CABINET: STYLE F
NAMEPLATE: STYLE 7

■ Black Tolex covering; silver grille.
■ Silverface control panel; Nine silver-top numbered knobs (Normal: bs, v, b, t. Vibrato: bs, v, b, t, s, i, r).
■ Speakers: 2 x 12in cabinet.
■ Valves: 3 x 7025, 2 x 12AT7, 12AX7, 2 x 6L6GC. Rectifier: 5U4GB.
■ Output: 45W.

From 1976 loses underlining on nameplate and gains master volume with distortion switch. Cabinet now has speakers mounted diagonally for compactness. JBLs an option. 1981 version raises output to 70W.

BANTAM BASS

1970-1972
CABINET: STYLE E
NAMEPLATE: STYLE 7

■ Black Tolex covering; silver grille.
■ Silverface control panel; Seven silver-top numbered knobs (Bass: ds, v, t, b. Normal: bs, v, t, m, b).
■ Yamaha plastic cone speaker.
■ Valves: 2 x 7025, 12AT7, 2 x 6L6, 5U4.
■ Output: 50W.
Bassman Ten with conventional speakers from 1973.

BASSMAN *TV front*

1951-1952
CABINET: STYLE B
NAMEPLATE: STYLE 1

■ Early tweed covering; cloth grille.
■ Top control panel (numbered); Two pointer knobs (v, t).
■ Speaker: 1 x 15 Jensen.
■ Valves: 2 x 6SJ7, 6N7 or 6SL7, 2 x 6L6.
■ Output: 26W.
Employs a closed back with circular ports. Unusually, the chassis is at the bottom of the cabinet instead of at the top.

BASSMAN *Wide panel*

1952-1954
CABINET: STYLE C
NAMEPLATE: STYLE 1

■ Diagonal tweed covering; cloth grille.
■ Top control panel (numbered); Two pointer knobs (v, t).
■ Speaker: 1 x 15 Jensen.
■ Valves: 2 x 6SJ7, 6SL7, 2 x 6L6.
■ Output: 26W.

BASSMAN *Narrow panel*

1954-1961
CABINET: STYLE D
NAMEPLATE: STYLE 3

■ Diagonal tweed covering; brown tweed-era grille.
■ Top control panel (numbered); Four pointer knobs (v, b, t, p).

■ Speakers: 4 x 10in Jensen.
■ Valves: 12 AY7, 2 x 12AX7, 2 x 6L6G, 2 x 5U4G.
■ Output: 50W.
From 1956, mid-range control added, four jacks and two volumes. Power valves changed to 2 x 5881. Rectifier changed to GZ34. The post 1956 Bassman is sometimes called the greatest of all instrument amps. More popular with guitarists than bassists.

BASSMAN *Brownface piggy-back*
	1961-1964
	CABINET: STYLE F
	NAMEPLATE: STYLE 6

■ Cream Tolex covering; maroon grille.
■ Brownface control panel (numbered); Seven brown knobs (v, t, b; v, t, b. Both: p).
■ Speaker: 1 x 12in Jensen.
■ Valves: 4 x 7025, 2 x 5881, GZ34.
■ Output: 50W.
Later models have silicon rectifiers, 3 x 7025, 12AT7 and 2 x 6L6GC valves. 2 x 12in cabinet introduced from 1962. Loses presence control and gets bright switch from 1964. Blackface from 1964.

BASSMAN *Blackface*
	1964-1968
	CABINET: STYLE F
	NAMEPLATE: STYLE 7

■ Black Tolex covering; silver grille.
■ Blackface control panel; Six silver-top numbered knobs (bs, v, t, b; bs, v, t, b).
■ Speakers: 2 x 12in Jensen.
■ Valves: 3 x 7025, 12AT7, 2 x 6L6GC, GZ34.
■ Output: 50W.

BASSMAN *Silverface*
	1968-1979
	CABINET: STYLE F
	NAMEPLATE: STYLE 7

■ Black Tolex covering; silver grille.
■ Silverface control panel; Six silver-top numbered knobs (Deep: v, t, b; normal: v, t b).
■ Speakers: 2 x 12in Jensen.
■ Valves: 3 x 7025, 12AT7, 2 x 6L6GC, GZ34.
■ Output: 50W.
2 x 15in cabinet from 1970. Renamed Bassman 50 from about 1972. Nameplate loses underlining from 1976.

'59 BASSMAN *Vintage re-issue*
	INTRODUCED 1990
	CABINET: STYLE D
	NAMEPLATE: STYLE 3

■ Diagonal tweed covering; brown tweed-era grille.
■ Top control panel (numbered); Five pointer knobs (Normal v, bright v, t, m, b).
■ Speakers: 4 x 10in.
■ Valves: 3 x 12AX7, 2 x 6L6, silicon rectifier.
■ Output: 45W.
Reissue of 1959 tweed Bassman. A 5U4G valve rectifier is an option.

BASSMAN COMPACT
	1981-1985
	CABINET: STYLE E
	NAMEPLATE: STYLE 9

■ Black Tolex covering; silver grille.
■ New blackface control panel; Six silver-top numbered knobs (v, t, m, b, compressor, master v).
■ Speaker: 1 x 15in.
■ Solid state.
■ Output: 50W.

BASSMAN SOLID STATE *See* **SOLID STATE**

BASSMAN TEN
	1972-1982
	CABINET: STYLE E
	NAMEPLATE: STYLE 7.

■ Black Tolex covering; silver grille.
■ Silverface control panel; Eight silver-top numbered knobs (Bass: ds, v, t, b; Normal: bs, v, t, m. b. Master v).
■ Speakers: 4 x 10in.
■ Valves: 2 x 7025, 12AT7, 2 x 6L6GC, silicon rectifiers.
■ Output: 50W.
New blackface from 1981. Uprated to 70W in 1981.

BASSMAN 20
	1982-85
	CABINET: STYLE E
	NAMEPLATE: STYLE 9

■ Black Tolex covering; silver grille.
■ New blackface control panel; Four silver-top numbered knobs (v, t, m, b).
■ Speaker: 1 x 15in.
■ Valves: 2 x 7025, 2 x 6V6GTA.
■ Output: 20W.
A relative of the 1982 Super Champ.

BASSMAN 50
	1972-1976
	CABINET: STYLE E
	NAMEPLATE: STYLE 7

■ Black Tolex covering; silver grille.
■ Silverface control panel; Six silver-top numbered knobs (Bass: ds, v, t, b; Normal: bs, v, t, b).
■ Speakers: 2 x 15in.
■ Valves: 2 x 7025, 12AT7, 2 x 6L6GC, silicon rectifiers.
■ Output: 50W.
Master volume 1974.

BASSMAN 60 (or Sidekick 60)
	1990-1994
	CABINET: STYLE E
	NAMEPLATE: STYLE 8

■ Black Tolex covering; silver grille.
■ Black control panel (numbered); Five black knobs (v, master, t, m, b).
■ Speaker: 1 x 15in.
■ Solid state.
■ Output: 60W.
Built by Fender Japan.

BASSMAN 70
	1977-1979
	CABINET: STYLE F
	NAMEPLATE: STYLE 8

■ Black Tolex covering; silver grille.
■ Silverface control panel; Seven silver-top numbered knobs (Bass: ds, v, t, b; Normal: bs, v, t, b. Master v).
■ Speakers: 2 x 15in cabinet.
■ Valves: 3 x 7025, 12AT7, 2 x 6L6GL, silicon rectifiers.
■ Output: 70W.

BASSMAN 100
	1972-1979
	CABINET: STYLE E
	NAMEPLATE: STYLE 7

■ Black Tolex covering; silver grille.
■ Silverface control panel; Eight silver-top numbered knobs (Bass: ds, v, t, b; Normal: bs, v, t, m, b. Master v).
■ Speakers: 4 x 12in.
■ Valves: 2 x 7025, 12AT7, 2 x 6L6.
■ Output: 100W.
Formerly Super Bassman. Later models lose underlining on nameplate.

BASSMAN 135

1979-1983
CABINET: STYLE F
NAMEPLATE: STYLE 8

- Black Tolex covering; silver grille.
- Silverface control panel; Nine silver-top numbered knobs (Bass: v, t, m, b; Normal: bs, v, t, m, b. Master v).
- Speakers: 4 x 10in cabinet.
- Valves: 2 x 7025, 12AT7, 4 x 6L6GC, silicon rectifiers.
- Output: 135W.

BLUES DE VILLE

INTRODUCED 1993
CABINET: STYLE D
NAMEPLATE: STYLE 2

- Diagonal tweed covering; brown tweed-era grille.
- Top control panel (numbered); Seven pointer knobs (v1, v2, b, m, t. P, r).
- Speakers: 4 x 10in.
- Valves: 3 x 12AX7, 2 x 6L6.
- Output: 60W.
1994: 2 x 12in version introduced.
A modern valve amp in tweed style.

BLUES DELUXE

INTRODUCED 1993
CABINET: STYLE D
NAMEPLATE: STYLE 2

- Diagonal tweed covering; brown tweed-era grille.
- Top control panel (numbered); Seven pointer knobs (v1, v2, b, m, t. P, r).
- Speaker: 1 x 12in.
- Valves: 3 x 12AX7, 2 x 6L6.
- Output: 40W.
Modern valve amp with tweed-era look.

BRONCO

1968-1974
CABINET: STYLE E
NAMEPLATE: STYLE 7

- Black Tolex covering; silver grille.
- Silverface control panel; Five silver-top numbered knobs (v, b, t, s, i).
- Speaker: 1 x 8in.
- Valves: 2 x 12AX7A, 6V6GTA.
- Output: 5W.
Power output raised to 6W in 1972.
Effectively the Vibro Champ with its name in red to match the Bronco student guitar. Schematics show it running at higher voltages than equivalent Vibro Champ, hence more headroom and output.

BRONCO

INTRODUCED 1993
CABINET: STYLE D
NAMEPLATE: STYLE 2

- Diagonal tweed covering; brown tweed-era grille.
- Top control panel (numbered); Three pointer knobs (v, b, t).
- Speaker: 1 x 8in.
- Solid state.
- Output: 15W.

BULLET

INTRODUCED 1993
CABINET: STYLE E
NAMEPLATE: STYLE 9

- Black Tolex covering; silver grille.
- Black control panel (numbered); Six black knobs (v, gain, v, t, m, b).
- Speaker: 1 x 8in.
- Solid state.
- Output: 15W.
Current starter model.

BXR DUAL BASS 400 HEAD

INTRODUCED 1987
CABINET: STYLE I
NAMEPLATE: NONE

- Black cloth on cabs.
- Black control panel (numbered); Four red knobs (gain, v, crossover balance & frequency) plus 11-band graphic eq.
- Various speakers.
- Solid state.
- Output: 2 x 200W.
Fender name is painted on front panel.

BXR15

INTRODUCED 1994
CABINET: STYLE J
NAMEPLATE: STYLE 8

- Black Tolex covering; black grille.
- Black control panel (numbered); Four black knobs (v, t, m, b).
- Speaker: 1 x 8in.
- Solid state.
- Output: 15W.
Derived from Squier SK15B.

BXR 25

INTRODUCED 1992
CABINET: STYLE J
NAMEPLATE: STYLE 9

- Black covering; black grille.
- Black control panel (numbered); Four black knobs (v, low, mid, high).
- Speaker: 1 x 10in.
- Solid state.
- Output: 25W.
Formerly R.A.D. Bass.

BXR 60

INTRODUCED 1994
CABINET: STYLE E
NAMEPLATE: STYLE 9

- Black Tolex covering; black grille.
- Black control panel (numbered); Five black knobs (v, four way eq).
- Speaker: 1 x 12in.
- Solid state.
- Output: 60W.
Announced mid 1994.

BXR 100

INTRODUCED 1993
CABINET: STYLE E
NAMEPLATE: STYLE 9

- Black Tolex covering; black grille.
- Black control panel (numbered); Three black knobs (v, two tones), plus seven-band graphic eq.
- Speaker: 1 x 15in.
- Solid state.
- Output: 100W.

BXR 300C

INTRODUCED 1987
CABINET: STYLE E
NAMEPLATE: STYLE 9

- Black Tolex covering; black grille.
- Black control panel (numbered); Five red knobs (v, t, mid, mid frequency, b).
- Speaker: 1 x 15in Eminence.
- Solid state.
- Output: 300W.
Also available as BXR300R rack system. Remodelled without red knobs 1993.

BXR 300R

INTRODUCED 1987
CABINET: STYLE I
NAMEPLATE: NONE

- Black control panel (numbered); Five red knobs (v, t, mid, mid frequency, b).
- Various speakers.
- Solid state.
- Output: 300W.

Also available as BXR300C combo. Remodelled without red knobs 1993. Fender name is painted on front panel.

CAPRICORN

1970-1972
CABINET: STYLE E
NAMEPLATE: STYLE 7

- Black Tolex covering; silver grille.
- Black/aluminium control panel; 10 numbered aluminium knobs (Normal: bs, v, t, b. Vibrato: bs, v, t, m, b, r, s, i).
- Speakers: 3 x 12in JBL.
- Solid state (28 transistors, 13 diodes).
- Output: 105W.

CHAMP *Wide panel*

1953-1954
CABINET: STYLE C
NAMEPLATE: STYLE 1

- Diagonal tweed covering; brown cloth grille.
- Black control panel (numbered); One pointer knob (v).
- Speaker: 1 x 6in Jensen.
- Valves: 6SJ7, 6V6, 5Y3.
- Output: 3W.

Called Student in catalogue. This is the Champion renamed: apparently there were other claimants to that name.

CHAMP *Narrow panel*

1954-1964
CABINET: STYLE D
NAMEPLATE: STYLE 1

- Tweed; brown tweed-era grille.
- Top control panel (numbered); One pointer knob (v).
- Speaker: 1 x 6in Jensen.
- Valves: 12AX7, 6V6GT, 5Y3GT.
- Output: 4W.

Some late narrow panel Champs come in black Tolex with black plastic handles.

CHAMP *Tolex*

1964-1979
CABINET: STYLE E
NAMEPLATE: NONE

- Black Tolex covering; silver grille.
- Blackface control panel; Three silver-top numbered knobs (v, t, b).
- Speaker: 1 x 8in.
- Valves: 12AX7, 6V6GT, 5YTGT.
- Output: 4W.

Output increased to 5W in 1965. Silverface from 1969. 6W output from 1972.
Grille-mounted badges come and go.

CHAMP II

1982-1985
CABINET: STYLE E
NAMEPLATE: STYLE 9

- Black Tolex covering; silver grille.
- New blackface control panel (numbered); Four silver-top numbered knobs (V, t, b, master v).
- Speaker: 1 x 10in.
- Valves: 2 x 7025, 2 x 6V6GTA, silicon rectifiers.
- Output: 18W.

Budget variant of the Super Champ.

CHAMP 12

1986-1992
CABINET: STYLE E
NAMEPLATE: STYLE 9

- Black Tolex covering; black grille.
- Black control panel (numbered); Six red knobs (t, b, v, overdrive gain, overdrive v, r).
- Speaker: 1 x 12in Eminence.
- Valves: 2 x 12AX6, 6L6.
- Output: 12W.

Made in USA by new Fender team.

CHAMP 25

INTRODUCED 1992
CABINET: STYLE J
NAMEPLATE: STYLE 7

- Black Tolex covering; black grille.
- Black control panel (numbered); Ten black knobs (Normal: v, t, m, b. Drive: gain, overdrive, t, b, v, r).
- Speaker: 1 x 12in.
- Valves: 2 x 5881/6L6 in power stage.
- Solid state pre-amp.
- Output: 25W.

Champ 25SE has master loudness control, standby switch and line and headphone outputs.
The new Fender company's first stab at a hybrid amp uses a valve power stage. This approach has since been abandoned.

CHAMPION 110

INTRODUCED 1993
CABINET: STYLE E
NAMEPLATE: STYLE 9

- Black Tolex covering; silver grille.
- Black control panel (numbered); Seven black knobs (v, overdrive gain, overdrive v, b, m, t, r).
- Speaker: 1 x 10in.
- Solid state.
- Output: 25W.

Footswitch for channel switching.

CHAMPION 600 *TV front*

1949-1953
CABINET: STYLE B
NAMEPLATE: STYLE 1

- Brown/cream covering; brown cloth grille.
- Black control panel (numbered); One pointer knob (v).
- Speaker: 1 x 6in Jensen.
- Valves: 6SJ7, 6V6, 5Y3.
- Output: 3W.

First of a long series. Derived from original grey crackle finish amps produced by K&F in mid-late 1940s. Also known as Student or Student 600.

CHAMPION 800 *TV front*

1948
CABINET: STYLE B
NAMEPLATE: STYLE 1

- Grey linen, grey cloth grille.
- Black control panel (numbered); One pointer knob (v).
- Speaker: 1 x 8in Jensen.
- Valves: 6SJ7, 6V6, 5Y3.
- Output: 4W.

Rarer 8in version of Champion. Only 100 made. Thought to predate Champion 600.

CONCERT *Brownface*

1960-1965
CABINET: STYLE E
NAMEPLATE: STYLE 6

- Brown Tolex covering; light brown grille.

■ Brownface control panel (numbered); Nine brown knobs (Normal: b, t, v. Vibrato: b, t, v, s, i. Both: p).
■ Speakers: 4 x 10in Jensen.
■ Valves: 5 x 7025, 2 x 6L6GC.
■ Output: 40W.
One 7025 is replaced by two 12AX7s and the 6L6GC valves by 5881 valves in 1962. It goes into blackface from 1964, loses the presence control and gains bright switches. The valves at that stage are 2 x 7025, 12AX7, 12AT7 and 2 x 6L6GC.
Another variant on the Pro/Super/Bandmaster chassis.

CONCERT Post CBS

INTRODUCED 1992
CABINET: STYLE E
NAMEPLATE: STYLE 7

■ Black Tolex covering; silver grille.
■ New blackface control panel; 12 silver-top numbered knobs (Ch 1: v, t, m, b. Ch 2: gain 1, gain 2, t, b, m, v. Both: mix, r).
■ Speaker: 1 x 12in.
■ Valves: 2 x 12AT7, 4 x 12AX7, 2 x 6L6.
■ Output: 60W.
Part of the current Pro Tube range. Derived from Super 60 of 1988.

CONCERT 112, 210, 410

1982-1985
CABINET: STYLE E
NAMEPLATE: STYLE 9

■ Black Tolex covering; silver grille.
■ New blackface control panel; 11 silver-top numbered knobs (Ch 1: v, t. Ch 2: v, gain, master, t, m, b, r, p).
■ Speakers: 1 x 12in, 2 x 10in or 4 x 10in.
■ Valves: 5 x 7025, 2 x 12AT7, 2 x 6L6GC.
■ Output: 60W.
1983: Concert Top and matching speaker cabinets. EV speakers are an option.
Modern amp with channel-switching and effects loop.

DELUXE Model 26

1946-1948
CABINET: STYLE A
NAMEPLATE: NONE

■ Polished wood; coloured felt with vertical chrome strips.
■ Back control panel (numbered); Three pointer knobs (Mic v, inst v, tone).
■ Speaker: 1 x 10in Jensen.
■ Valves: (early) 6SC7, 6N7, 2 x 6F6, 5Y3. (Later) 6V6 for 6F6.
■ Output: 10W.
Sometimes called the Model 26. The designation appears on the control panel of both Deluxe and Professional.

DELUXE TV front

1948-1952
CABINET: STYLE B
NAMEPLATE: STYLE 1

■ Early tweed covering; dark brown cloth grille.
■ Top control panel (numbered); Three pointer knobs (Mic v, inst v, tone).
■ Speaker: 1 x 12in Jensen.
■ Valves: 6SC7/6N7, 2 x 6V6, 5Y3.
■ Output: 10W.
Some have deep back panel.
Replacement for Model 26 style Deluxe.

DELUXE Wide panel

1952-1954
CABINET: STYLE C
NAMEPLATE: STYLE 1

■ Diagonal tweed covering; dark brown cloth grille.
■ Top control panel (numbered); Three pointer knobs (Mic v, inst v, tone).
■ Speaker: 1 x 12in Jensen.

■ Valves: 2 x 6SC7, 2 x 6V6, 5Y3.
■ Output: 10W.
Model numbers 5B3 and 5C3 are virtually identical. Some of model number 5D3, from about 1954, use miniature 12AX7 and 12AY7 pre-amp valves.

DELUXE Narrow panel

1954-1961
CABINET: STYLE D
NAMEPLATE: STYLE 2 or 3

■ Diagonal tweed covering; brown tweed-era grille.
■ Top control panel (numbered); Three pointer knobs (Mic v, inst v, tone).
■ Speaker: 1 x 12in Jensen.
■ Valves: 12AX7, 12AY7, 2 x 6V6, 5Y3.
■ Output: 15W.
Includes model numbers 5E3 and 5F3. The 5F3 has slightly higher voltages and gain.
Using only one half of a pre-amp valve as a phase inverter (instead of both halves in earlier models) means the other half can be used to provide higher gain. Deluxes are inclined to distort at quite low volume levels.

DELUXE Brownface

1961-1963
CABINET: STYLE E
NAMEPLATE: NONE

■ Brown Tolex covering; light brown grille.
■ Brownface control panel (numbered); Six brown knobs (Normal: v, t. Bright: v, t. Both: s, i).
■ Speaker: 1 x 12in Jensen.
■ Valves: 7025, 2 x 12AX7, 2 x 6V6, GZ34.
■ Output: 15W.
All brown Tolex Deluxes include tremolo, which operates initially on the power section and hence both channels.

DELUXE Blackface

1963/4-1966
CABINET: STYLE E
NAMEPLATE: NONE

■ Black Tolex covering; silver grille.
■ Blackface control panel: Eight silver-top numbered knobs (Normal: v, b, t. Vibrato: v, b, t, s, i).
■ Speaker: 1 x 12in Jensen.
■ Valves: 2 x 7025, 12AX7, 12AY7, 2 x 6V6, GZ34. Output: 20W.
Model numbers AA763 and AB763 are virtually identical. Some get underlined Fender nameplate on grille from about 1966.
Black Tolex covering Deluxes include separate bass and treble controls and a tremolo circuit that operates only on one channel. Effectively superceded by Deluxe Reverb, which was introduced in 1963.

DELUXE 85

1988-1993
CABINET: STYLE E
NAMEPLATE: STYLE 9

■ Black Tolex covering; black grille.
■ Black control panel (numbered); 11 red knobs (Ch A: v, t, b. Ch B: gain, b, m, t, limiter, p, r, v).
■ Speaker: 1 x 12in Eminence.
■ Solid state.
■ Output: 65W.
The current Fender regime's first attempt at solid state.
Now discontinued.

DELUXE 112

INTRODUCED 1992
CABINET: STYLE E
NAMEPLATE: STYLE 9

■ Black Tolex covering; silver grille.
■ Black control panel (numbered); Ten black knobs (Normal: v, t, m, b. Drive: gain, contour, t, b, v, r).

■ Speaker: 1 x 12in.
■ Solid state.
■ Output: 65W.
A derivative of the Deluxe 85, simplified and made more traditional in appearance.

DELUXE REVERB *Blackface*

1963/4-1968
CABINET: STYLE E
NAMEPLATE: NONE

■ Black Tolex covering; silver grille.
■ Blackface control panel; Nine silver-top numbered knobs (Normal: v, b, t. Vibrato: v, b, t, r, s, i).
■ Speaker: 1 x 12in.
■ Valves: 3 x 7025, 2 x 12AT7, 12AX7, 2 x 6V6, GZ34.
■ Output: 20W.
Fender nameplate on grille from about 1966.
Black Tolex covering Deluxes include separate bass and treble controls and a tremolo circuit that operates only on one channel.

DELUXE REVERB *Silverface*

1968-c1979
CABINET: STYLE E
NAMEPLATE: STYLE 7

■ Black Tolex covering; silver grille.
■ Silverface control panel; Nine silver-top numbered knobs (Normal: v, b, t. Vibrato: v, b, t, r, s, i).
■ Speaker: 1 x 12in.
■ Valves: 3 x 7025, 2 x 12AT7, 12AX7, 2 x 6V6.
■ Output: 20W.
This amp remained virtually unchanged for more than 10 years. Nameplate loses underlining in 1976.
This silverface Deluxe reverb is very similar to the blackface version. A 1200 pF capacitor was placed on the grids of each of the power valves to cure instability, with some effect on treble output.

'65 DELUXE REVERB *Vintage reissue*

INTRODUCED 1993
CABINET: STYLE E
NAMEPLATE: STYLE 7

■ Black Tolex covering; silver grille.
■ Blackface control panel; Nine silver-top numbered knobs (Normal: v, b, t. Vibrato: v, b, t, r, s, i).
■ Speaker: 1 x 12in.
■ Valves: 3 x 12AX7, 2 x 12AT7, 2 x 6V6, 5AR4.
■ Output: 22W.
Reissue of pre-CBS Deluxe Reverb in Vintage series.

DELUXE REVERB SOLID STATE
See SOLID STATE

DELUXE REVERB II

1982-1985
CABINET: STYLE E
NAMEPLATE: STYLE 9

■ Black Tolex covering; silver grille.
■ New blackface control panel; 11 silver-top numbered knobs (Ch 1: v, t, b. Ch 2: v, gain, master, t, m, b, r, p).
■ Speaker: 1 x 12in.
■ Valves: 5 x 7025, 12AT7, 2 x 6V6GTA.
■ Solid state rectifier.
■ Output: 20W.
All new switchable channel version of Deluxe Reverb. A product of the Paul Rivera era.

DUAL PROFESSIONAL *V-front*

1946-1947
CABINET: V-FRONT COMBO
NAMEPLATE: STYLE 1

Early tweed covering; dark brown grille with chrome strip.

■ Top control panel (numbered); Three pointer knobs (mic v, inst v, tone).
■ Speakers: 2 x 10in Jensen.
■ Valves: 3 x 6SJ7, 2 x 6L6, 5U4.
■ Output: 16W.
First two speaker amplifier. Renamed Super.

DUAL PROFESSIONAL *Custom Shop*

ANNOUNCED 1994
CABINET: STYLE E
NAMEPLATE: STYLE 6

■ Cream Tolex covering; black grille.
■ Brownface control panel (numbered); Ten cream knobs (Ch 1: v, t, b. Ch 2: v, t, m, b, both: r, s, i).
■ Speakers: 3 x 10in with AlNiCo magnets.
■ Valves: TBA.
■ Output: 100W.
High powered reverb version of Vibro-King.

DUAL SHOWMAN *Post CBS version*

1987-1994
CABINET: STYLE F
NAMEPLATE: STYLE 9

■ Black Tolex covering; black grille.
■ Black control panel (numbered); Ten red knobs (Ch 1: v, t, m, b. Ch 2: gain, t, m, b, p, v).
■ Choice of cabinets.
■ Valves: 4 x 12AX7, 1 x 12AT7, 4 x 6L6GC.
■ Output: 100W.
Red knob/black grille replaced in 1992 by more traditional look. Also available with reverb.

DUAL SHOWMAN *See also* SHOWMAN

DUAL SHOWMAN REVERB *Silverface*

1969-1979
CABINET: STYLE F
NAMEPLATE: STYLE 7

■ Black Tolex covering; silver grille.
■ Silverface control panel; 11 silver-top numbered knobs (Normal: bs, v, b, m, t. Vibrato: bs, v, b, m, t, s, i, r).
■ Speakers: 2 x 15in JBL.
■ Valves: 3 x 7025, 2 x 12AT7, 12 AX7, 4 x 6L6GC.
■ Output: 100W.
1972 master volume. 1976 master volume and distortion switch. Also sold as Dual Showman Reverb Bass.

HARVARD

1956-1961
CABINET: STYLE D
NAMEPLATE: STYLE 3 or 5

■ Diagonal tweed covering; brown tweed-era grille.
■ Top control panel (numbered); Two pointer knobs (v, tone).
■ Speaker: 1 x 8in.
■ Valves: 6AT6, 12AX7, 2 x 6V6, 5Y3.
■ Output: 10W.
From 1958/9 Harvard has a 10in speaker. The final models have a single 12AX7 and a single 6V6GT, making them less powerful than the Princeton.
The Harvard was destined to clash with the Princeton and Champ at the bottom end of the range. Discontinued 1961.

HARVARD *Solid state*

1979-1982
CABINET: STYLE E
NAMEPLATE: STYLE 8

■ Black Tolex covering; silver grille.
■ New blackface control panel; Four silver-top numbered knobs (v, b, t, master v).
■ Speaker: 1 x 10in.

■ Solid state.
■ Output: 20W.
Also Harvard Reverb.
Short-lived transistor budget amp.

HARVARD REVERB II

1982-1985
CABINET: STYLE E
NAMEPLATE: STYLE 9

■ Black Tolex covering; silver grille.
■ New blackface control panel; Seven silver-top numbered knobs
(v, gain, master, t, m, b, r).
■ Speaker: 1 x 10in.
■ Solid state.
■ Output: 20W.
Low price single channel transistor amp.

H.O.T.

INTRODUCED 1990
CABINET: STYLE J
NAMEPLATE: STYLE 9

■ Grey carpet covering; black grille.
■ Black control panel (numbered); Three red knobs (contour, v, t).
■ Speaker: 1 x 10in.
■ Solid state.
■ Output: 25W.
Remodelled with black covering and black knobs from 1992.
Tone control is via switches.

J.A.M.

INTRODUCED 1990
CABINET: STYLE J
NAMEPLATE: STYLE 9

■ Grey carpet covering; black grille.
■ Black control panel (numbered); Five red knobs (contour, v, r,
chorus rate and depth).
■ Speaker: 1 x 12in.
■ Solid state.
■ Output: 25W.
Remodelled with black covering and black knobs from 1992.
Tone control is via switches.

K&F

1945-1946
CABINET: STYLE A
NAMEPLATE: K&F

■ Grey crackle paint; coarse mesh or cloth.
■ No controls or one knob (v).
■ Speakers: 1 x 8in or 1 x 10in.
■ Valves: 6N7, 6V6, 5Y3.
■ Output: 3W.
Found with two different sized speakers.
The first amplifier produced by Leo Fender. For use with lap steel type
guitar. Extremely rare.

LIBRA

1970-1972
CABINET: STYLE E
NAMEPLATE: STYLE 7

■ Black/aluminium control panel; Ten aluminium numbered knobs
(Normal: bs, v, t, b. Vibrato: bs, v, t, m, b, r, s, i).
■ Speakers: 4 x 12in JBL.
■ Solid state (28 transistors, 13 diodes).
■ Output: 105W.

LONDON REVERB SERIES

1983-1985
CABINET: STYLE E or F
NAMEPLATE: STYLE 9

■ Black Tolex covering; silver grille.
■ New blackface control panel: 12 silver-top numbered knobs
(Ch 1: v, t, b. Ch 2: v, gain, master, t, mid 1, mid 2, b, r1, r2)
plus 5-way eq.
■ Speakers: 1 x 12in or 2 x 10in.
■ Solid state.
■ Output: 100W.
London Reverb 112 and 210 are combos. London Reverb Top is the
piggy back version.
Extremely elaborate solid state amps.

LONDON 185

1988-1992
CABINET: STYLE F
NAMEPLATE: STYLE 9

■ Black Tolex covering; black grille.
■ Black control panel (numbered); 12 red knobs (Ch 1: v, t, b.
Ch 2: gain, boost, t, m, b, contour, p, r, v).
■ Various speakers.
■ Solid state.
■ Output: 160W.
Head version of 185-type solid state amp to be used with Celestion
speakers for pseudo-British sound.

M-80

INTRODUCED 1990
CABINET: STYLE J or F
NAMEPLATE: STYLE 9

■ Grey carpet covering; black grille.
■ Black control panel (numbered); Nine red knobs (Clean: v, t, m, b.
Overdrive: v, gain, contour, p, v).
■ Speakers: 1 x 12in or 2 x 12in.
■ Solid state.
■ Output: 90W.
Available in combo, chorus combo, head, chorus head and Pro head
versions with matching speaker cabinets. Chorus 2 x 65W stereo
output. Whole range remodelled with black covering and black knobs
from 1992.

M-80 BASS

INTRODUCED 1991
CABINET: STYLE J
NAMEPLATE: STYLE 9

■ Grey carpet covering; black grille.
■ Black control panel (numbered); Six red knobs (v, t, m, b, chorus
rate and depth).
■ Speakers: 1 x 15in.
■ Solid state.
■ Output: 160W.
Also available as head and cab with 2 x 15in speakers.
Later remodelled in black with black knobs.

MODEL 26 See DELUXE Model 26

MONTREUX

1983-1985
CABINET: STYLE E
NAMEPLATE: STYLE 9

■ Black Tolex covering; silver grille.
■ New blackface control panel; 12 silver-top numbered knobs
(Ch 1: v, t, b. Ch 2: v, gain, master, t, mid 1, mid 2, b, r1, r2).
■ Speaker: 1 x 12in.
■ Solid state.
■ Output: 100W.

MUSICMASTER BASS

1970-1983
CABINET: STYLE E
NAMEPLATE: STYLE 7

■ Black Tolex covering; silver grille.

■ Silverface control panel; Two numbered aluminium knobs (v, tone).
■ Speaker: 1 x 12in.
■ Valves: 12AX7A, 2 x 6V6GTA.
■ Output: 12W.
*Later models have front on/off switch and standard silverface knobs.
New blackface look from 1979.*

PERFORMER 1000

INTRODUCED 1993
CABINET: STYLE E
NAMEPLATE: STYLE 9

■ Black Tolex covering; silver grille.
■ New blackface control panel; 11 black knobs (Ch 1: v, t, m, b.
Ch 2: gain, t, m, b, volume. Both: r and effects mix).
■ Speaker: 1 x 12in.
■ Valves: 12AX7 in pre-amp, otherwise Solid state.
■ Output: 100W.
*Also available in piggy-back version with 1 x 12in or 4 x 12in speakers.
Second stab at hybrid design. The first was Champ 25.*

POWER CHORUS

INTRODUCED 1991
CABINET: STYLE E
NAMEPLATE: STYLE 9

■ Black Tolex covering; black grille.
■ Black control panel (numbered); 15 red knobs (Ch 1: v, t, m, b.
Ch 2: gain, boost, t, m, b, contour, p, v, r, chorus rate and depth).
■ Speakers: 2 x 12in Eminence.
■ Solid state.
■ Output: 2 x 65W.
US-built chorus amp. Later remodelled as Ultra Chorus.

PRINCETON *Model 26 style*

1946-1948
CABINET: STYLE A
NAMEPLATE: NONE

■ Polished wood; coloured cloth with chrome strips.
■ No control panel; jack socket only.
■ Speaker: 1 x 8in Jensen or Utah.
■ Valves: 6SL7, 6V6, 5Y3.
■ Output 4.5W.
Also known as Student (as was the Champion).

PRINCETON *TV front*

1948-1952
CABINET: STYLE B
NAMEPLATE: STYLE 1

■ Early tweed covering; brown cloth grille.
■ Top control panel (numbered); Two pointer knobs (v, tone).
■ Speaker: 1 x 8in Jensen.
■ Valves: 6SL7, 6V6, 5Y3.
■ Output: 4.5W.

PRINCETON *Wide panel*

1952-1954
CABINET: STYLE C
NAMEPLATE: STYLE 1

■ Diagonal tweed covering; brown cloth grille.
■ Top control panel (numbered); Two pointer knobs (v, tone).
■ Speaker: 1 x 8in Jensen.
■ Valves: 6SL7, 6V6, 5Y3.
■ Output: 4.5W.
*Pre-amp valve becomes 6SC7 from 1953 and 12AX7 from 1954.
Some 200 Princetons were cannibalised into the first Mesa Boogies.*

PRINCETON *Narrow panel*

1954-1961
CABINET: STYLE D
NAMEPLATE: STYLE 2, 3 or 4

■ Diagonal tweed covering; brown tweed-era grille.

■ Top control panel (numbered); Two pointer knobs (v, tone).
■ Speaker: 1 x 8in Jensen.
■ Valves: 12AX7, 6V6, 5Y3.
■ Output: 4.5W.
*After 1956, various Fender script nameplate styles are used, some
including the model name.
Some 200 Princetons were cannibalised into the first Mesa Boogies.*

PRINCETON *Brownface/Blackface*

1961-1969
CABINET: STYLE E
NAMEPLATE: NONE

■ Brown Tolex covering; light brown grille.
■ Brownface control panel (numbered); Four brown knobs (v, tone, s, i).
■ Speaker: 1 x 10in Jensen.
■ Valves: 7025, 12AX7, 2 x 6V6, 5Y3.
■ Output: 12W.
*Black Tolex from 1963, with black or white knobs. Separate bass and
treble controls from mid 1964. Underlined nameplate from about 1966.
The Tolex Princetons have a tremolo circuit, a push-pull power stage
and 12W output.*

PRINCETON *Silverface*

1969-1979
CABINET: STYLE E
NAMEPLATE: STYLE 7

■ Black Tolex covering; silver grille.
■ Silverface control panel; Four silver-top numbered knobs (v, tone, s,
i).
■ Speaker: 1 x 10in Jensen.
■ Valves: 7025, 12AX7, 2 x 6V6, 5Y3.
■ Output: 12W.
*Identical to late blackface version. Virtually unchanged internally
through last 15 years of life.*

PRINCETON CHORUS *Post-CBS*

INTRODUCED 1989
CABINET: STYLE E
NAMEPLATE: STYLE 9

■ Black Tolex covering; black grille.
■ Black control panel (numbered); 11 red knobs (v, t, m, b, r, gain,
limiter, p, v, chorus rate & depth).
■ Speakers: 2 x 10in Eminence.
■ Solid state.
■ Output: 2 x 25W (stereo).
*Revised with black knobs and silver grille from 1992.
US built chorus amp was a major departure.*

PRINCETON REVERB *Blackface*

1964-1969
CABINET: STYLE E
NAMEPLATE: NONE

■ Black Tolex covering; silver grille.
■ Blackface control panel; Six silver-top numbered knobs (v, t, b, r, s, i).
■ Speaker: 1 x 10in.
■ Valves: 7025, 2 x 12AX7, 12AT7, 2 x 6V6, 5U4.
■ Output: 12W.
Raised underlined Fender nameplate on grille from 1966.

PRINCETON REVERB *Silverface*

1969-1979
CABINET: STYLE E
NAMEPLATE: STYLE 7

■ Black Tolex covering; silver grille.
■ Silverface control panel; Six silver-top numbered knobs (v, t, b, r, s, i).
■ Speaker: 1 x 10in.
■ Valves: 7025, 2 x 12AX7, 12AT7, 2 x 6V6, 5U4.
■ Output: 12W.
*Nameplate loses underlining in 1976. Valves changed to 3 x 7025,
12AT7 and 2 x 6V6GTA in 1977.*

PRINCETON REVERB II

1982-1985
CABINET: STYLE E
NAMEPLATE: STYLE 9

▪ Black Tolex covering; silver grille.
▪ New blackface control panel; Eight silver-top numbered knobs (v, t, m, b, r, lead level, master v, p).
▪ Speaker: 1 x 12in.
▪ Valves: 3 x 7025, 12AT7, 2 x 6V6.
▪ Solid state.
▪ Output: 20W.
Pull switch gives overdriven lead sound through multiple gain controls.

PRINCETON 112 *Post-CBS*

INTRODUCED 1993
CABINET: STYLE E
NAMEPLATE: STYLE 9

▪ Black Tolex covering; silver grille.
▪ Black control panel (numbered); Nine black knobs (Normal: v, t, b. Drive: gain, contour, t, b, r).
▪ Speaker: 1 x 12in.
▪ Solid state.
▪ Output: 40W.
Part of the new Standard range.

PRO AMP *TV front*

1948-1952
CABINET: STYLE B
NAMEPLATE: STYLE 1

▪ Early tweed covering; brown cloth grille.
▪ Top control panel (numbered); Three pointer knobs (mic v, inst v, tone).
▪ Speaker: 1 x 15in Jensen.
▪ Valves: 3 x 6SC7, 2 x 6L6G, 5U4G.
▪ Output: c15W.
Formerly the Professional.

PRO AMP *Wide panel*

1952-1954
CABINET: STYLE C
NAMEPLATE: STYLE 1

▪ Diagonal tweed covering; brown cloth grille.
▪ Top control panel (numbered); Three pointer knobs (mic v, inst v, tone).
▪ Speaker: 1 x 15in Jensen.
▪ Valves: 12AY7, 12AX7, 2 x 6L6G, 5U5G.
▪ Output: 15W.

PRO AMP *Narrow panel*

1954-1960
CABINET: STYLE D
NAMEPLATE: STYLE 2

▪ Diagonal tweed covering; brown tweed-era grille.
▪ Top control panel (numbered); Three pointer knobs (mic volume, inst volume, tone).
▪ Speaker: 1 x 15in Jensen.
▪ Valves: 2 x 12AY7, 12AX7, 2 x 6L6, 5U5G.
▪ Output: 26W.
Nameplate 3 from about 1957.

PRO AMP *Brownface*

1960-1963
CABINET: STYLE D
NAMEPLATE: STYLE 6

▪ Brown Tolex covering; light brown grille.
▪ Brownface control panel (numbered); Nine brown knobs (Normal: v, t, b, s, i. Vibrato: v,t,b. Both: p).
▪ Speaker: 1 x 15in Jensen.
▪ Valves: 5 x 7025, 2 x 6L6GC.
▪ Output: 25W.
Late 1960-61, change to 4 x 7025, 2 x 12AX7, 2 x 5881.

PRO AMP *Blackface*

1963-1965
CABINET: STYLE E
NAMEPLATE: STYLE 7

▪ Black Tolex covering; silver grille.
▪ Blackface control panel; Eight silver-top numbered knobs (Normal: bs, v, t, b; Vibrato: bs, v, t, b, s, i).
▪ Speaker: 1 x 15in.
▪ Valves: 2 x 7025, 12AX7, 12AT7, 6L6GC, GZ34.
▪ Output: 25W.
Disappears after arrival of Pro Reverb.

PRO JUNIOR

INTRODUCED 1994
CABINET: STYLE D
NAMEPLATE: STYLE 2

▪ Diagonal tweed covering; brown tweed-era grille.
▪ Top control panel (numbered); Two pointer knobs (v, tone).
▪ Speaker: 1 x 10in.
▪ Valves: 2 x 12AX7, 2 x EL84.
▪ Output: 15W.
Not unlike an early Champ or Princeton to look at, but with very different valves.

PRO REVERB *Blackface*

1965-1969
CABINET: STYLE E
NAMEPLATE: STYLE 7

▪ Black Tolex covering; silver grille.
▪ Blackface control panel; Nine silver-top numbered knobs (Normal: bs, v, t, b; Vibrato: bs, v, t, b, r, s, i).
▪ Speakers: 2 x 12in.
▪ Valves: 3 x 7025, 12AX7, 2 x 12AT7, 2 x 6L6G, 5U4GB.
▪ Output: 40W.

PRO REVERB *Silverface*

1969-1982
CABINET: STYLE E
NAMEPLATE: STYLE 7

▪ Black Tolex covering; silver grille.
▪ Silverface control panel; Nine silver-top numbered knobs (Normal: bs, v, t, b. Vibrato: bs, v, 5, b, r, s, i).
▪ Speakers: 2 x 12in.
▪ Valves: 3 x 7025, 12AX7, 2 x 12AT7, 2 x 6L6GC, GZ34.
▪ Output: 40W.
45W output from 1972, achieved by different rectifier and increased anode voltage in output stage. 1976, master volume and pull distortion switch added. New blackface look from c1980.

PRO REVERB *New blackface*

1981
CABINET: STYLE E
NAMEPLATE: STYLE 9

▪ Black Tolex covering; silver grille.
▪ New blackface control panel; 12 silver-top numbered knobs (Normal: bs, v, t, m, b. Vibrato: bs, v, t, m, b, r, s, i, master v with pull distortion).
▪ Speakers: 2 x 12in.
▪ Valves: 4 x 7025, 2 x 12AT7, 2 x 6L6.
▪ Output: 70W.
Last of the line.

PRO REVERB SOLID STATE
See SOLID STATE

PRO 185 *Post-CBS*

INTRODUCED 1989
CABINET: STYLE E
NAMEPLATE: STYLE 9

▪ Black Tolex covering; black grille.

■ Black control panel (numbered); 14 red knobs (Ch A: v, t, m, b. Ch B: gain, gain boost, t, m, b, mid boost, contour, tilt, p, r).
■ Speakers: 2 x 12in Eminence.
■ Solid state.
■ Output: 160W.
Red knob style replaced by black knobs and silver grille by 1993.

PROFESSIONAL AMP Model 26 style

1946-1948
CABINET: STYLE A
NAMEPLATE: NONE

■ Polished wood; coloured felt grille with chrome strips.
■ Back control panel (numbered); Three pointer knobs (mic v, inst v, tone).
■ Speaker: 1 x 15in Jensen.
■ Valves: 6SC7/6N7. Power: 2 x 6L6, 5Y3.
■ Output: 15W.
A variant of the Model 26, but with a 15in speaker. Note that some of these use a field coil speaker, which has no permanent magnet.

QUAD REVERB

1970-1979
CABINET: STYLE E
NAMEPLATE: STYLE 7

■ Black Tolex covering; silver grille.
■ Silverface control panel; 12 silver-top numbered knobs (Normal: bs, v,-t, m, b. Vibrato: bs, v, t, m, b, r, s, i. master v).
■ Speakers: 4 x 12in.
■ Valves: 3 x 7025, 2 x 12AT7, 12AX7A, 4 x 6L6GC.
■ Output: 100W.
1976 has distortion switch on master volume control.
The Twin Reverb in a different guise.

R.A.D.

INTRODUCED 1990
CABINET: STYLE J
NAMEPLATE: STYLE 9

■ Grey carpet covering; black grille.
■ Black control panel (numbered); Two red knobs (contour, v).
■ Speaker: 1 x 8in.
■ Solid state.
■ Output: 20W.
Remodelled with black carpet covering and black knobs from 1992.
Tone control is via switches.

R.A.D. BASS

INTRODUCED 1992
CABINET: STYLE J
NAMEPLATE: STYLE 9

■ Grey carpet covering; black grille.
■ Black control panel (numbered); four red knobs (v, low, mid, high).
■ Speaker: 1 x 10in.
■ Solid state.
■ Output: 25W.
1992: remodelled in black with black knobs.
From 1994, renamed and repackaged as BXR 25.

SCORPIO

1970-1972
CABINET: STYLE E
NAMEPLATE: STYLE 7

■ Black Tolex covering; silver grille.
■ Black/aluminium control panel; 10 numbered aluminium knobs (Normal: bs, v, t, b. Vibrato: bs, v, t, m, b, r, s, i).
■ Speakers: 2 x 12in JBL.
■ Solid state.
■ Output: 56W.

SHOWMAN (and DUAL SHOWMAN)
Piggy-back

1961-1969
CABINET: STYLE F
NAMEPLATE: STYLE 6

■ Cream Tolex covering; maroon grille.
■ Brownface control panel (numbered); Nine white or brown knobs (Normal: v, t, b. Vibrato: v, t, b, s, i. Both: p).
■ Speakers: 1 x 12in or 1 x 15in JBL.
■ Valves: 4 x 7025, 2 x 12AX7, 4 x 5881.
■ Output: 85W.
Early versions use 6 x 7025 and 4 x 6L6GC. From 1964, blackface control layout is used, with bright switches and no presence control. Valves become 2 x 7025, 12AT7, 12AX7 and 4 x 6L6GC. Dual Showman is same amplifier with 2 x 15in JBLs. Whole line is in black Tolex from August 1964. Silverface from 1969.
The Showman is essentially a piggy-back version of the Twin.

SHOWMAN 112, 212, 115, 210

1983-1985
CABINET: STYLE E
NAMEPLATE: STYLE 9

■ Black Tolex covering; silver grille.
■ New blackface control panel; 12 silver-top numbered knobs (Ch 1: v, t, b. Ch 2: v, gain, master, t, mid 1, mid 2, b, r1, r2) plus 5-way graphic eq.
■ Speakers: 1 x 12in, 2 x 12in, 1 x 15in or 2 x 10in.
■ Solid state.
■ Output: 200W.
High power solid state amps with exceptionally complex controls.

SIDEKICK BASS (or Squier SK Bass)

1988-1993
CABINET: STYLE E
NAMEPLATE: STYLE 8

■ Black Tolex covering; silver grille.
■ Black control panel (numbered); Five black knobs (v, master, t, m, b).
■ Speaker: 1 x 10in.
■ Solid state.
■ Output: 30W.
Called Bassman 30 by Japanese. Sometimes called SK Bass.
Made by Fender Japan.

SIDEKICK BASSMAN

1989-1994
CABINET: STYLE E
NAMEPLATE: STYLE 8

■ Black Tolex covering; silver grille.
■ Black control panel (numbered); Six black knobs (v, master, t, m, b, limiter).
■ Speaker: 1 x 15in.
■ Solid state.
■ Output: 60W.
Also called Bassman 60.
Made by Fender Japan.

SIDEKICK KEYBOARD
(or Squier SK Keyboard)

1988-1994
CABINET: STYLE E
NAMEPLATE: STYLE 8

■ Black Tolex covering; silver grille.
■ Black control panel (numbered); Six black knobs (v1, v2, t, m, b, master).
■ Speaker: 1 x 10in.
■ Solid state.
■ Output: 30W.
Some have raised Squier nameplate on grille.
Made by Fender Japan.

SIDEKICK KEYBOARD 60

1989-1994
CABINET: STYLE E
NAMEPLATE: STYLE 8

■ Black Tolex covering; silver grille.
■ Black control panel (numbered); 11 black knobs (v1, v2, v3, r1, r2, r3, t, mid 1, mid 2, b, master).
■ Speakers: 12in and 4.5in.
■ Solid state.
■ Output: 30W.
Known as Keyman 60 in Japan.
Made by Fender Japan.

SIDEKICK REVERB 20

1983-1985
CABINET: STYLE E
NAMEPLATE: STYLE 8

■ Black Tolex covering; silver grille.
■ New blackface control panel; Six black knobs (v, master, t, m, b, r).
■ Speaker: 1 x 10in.
■ Solid state.
■ Output: 20W.
Made by Fender Japan.

SIDEKICK REVERB 30

1983-1985
CABINET: STYLE E
NAMEPLATE: STYLE 8

■ Black Tolex covering; silver grille.
■ New blackface control panel; seven silver-top numbered knobs (V, master, t, m, b, p, r).
■ Speaker: 1 x 12in.
■ Solid state.
■ Output: 30W.
Includes effects loop.
Made by Fender Japan.

SIDEKICK SWITCHER
(or Squier SK Switcher)

1988-1989
CABINET: STYLE E
NAMEPLATE: STYLE 8

■ Black Tolex covering; silver grille.
■ Black control panel (numbered); 11 black knobs (Ch 1: v, t, b. Ch 2: v, gain, master, t, b, m, p, r).
■ Speaker: 1 x 12in.
■ Solid state.
■ Output: 35W.
Sometimes called Fender Switcher. Some have raised Squier nameplate on grille. Some made in Taiwan.

SIDEKICK 10

1983-1985
CABINET: STYLE E
NAMEPLATE: STYLE 8

■ Black Tolex covering; silver grille.
■ New blackface control panel; Five black knobs (v, master, t, m, b).
■ Speaker: 1 x 8in.
■ Solid state.
■ Output: 10W.
Made by Fender Japan.

SIDEKICK 15R (or Squier SK15R)

1986-1992
CABINET: STYLE E
NAMEPLATE: STYLE 8

■ Black Tolex covering; silver grille.
■ Black control panel (numbered); Seven black knobs (v, gain, master, t, m, b, r).

■ Speaker: 1 x 8in.
■ Solid state.
■ Output: 15W.
Variant of Fender Japan's Sidekick 15R. Some have raised Squier badge on grille.

SIDEKICK 25 REVERB
(or Squier SK25R)

1986-1992
CABINET: STYLE E
NAMEPLATE: STYLE 8

■ Black Tolex covering; silver grille.
■ Black control panel (numbered); Eight black knobs (v, gain, master, t, m, b, p, r).
■ Speaker: 1 x 10in.
■ Solid state.
■ Output: 25W.
Also known as Squier Sidekick 25R, with raised Squier nameplate on grille.
Made by Fender Japan.

SIDEKICK 30 BASS

1983-1985
CABINET: STYLE E
NAMEPLATE: STYLE 8

■ Black Tolex covering; silver grille.
■ New blackface; Six black numbered knobs (V, master, t, m, b, p).
■ Speaker: 1 x 12in.
■ Solid state.
■ Output: 30W.

SIDEKICK 35 BASS

1986-1989
CABINET: STYLE E
NAMEPLATE: STYLE 8

■ Black Tolex covering; silver grille.
■ Black control panel. (numbered); Six black knobs (Gain, t, m, frequency, b, master).
■ Speaker: 1 x 12in.
■ Solid state.
■ Output: 35W.
Made by Fender Japan.

SIDEKICK 35 REVERB

1986-1990
CABINET: STYLE E
NAMEPLATE: STYLE 8

■ Black Tolex covering; silver grille.
■ Black control panel (numbered); Seven black knobs (v, gain, master, t, m, b, p, r).
■ Speaker: 1 x 12in.
■ Solid state.
■ Output: 35W.
Also known as Squier Sidekick 35R. Some have raised Squier nameplate on grille.
Made by Fender Japan.

SIDEKICK 50 BASS

1983-1985
CABINET: STYLE E
NAMEPLATE: STYLE 8

■ Black Tolex covering; silver grille.
■ New blackface control panel; Six black numbered knobs (v, master, t, m, b, p).
■ Speaker: 1 x 15in.
■ Solid state.
■ Output: 50W.
Made by Fender Japan.

SIDEKICK 60 *See* BASSMAN 60

SIDEKICK 65 BASS

1986-1989	
CABINET: STYLE E	
NAMEPLATE: STYLE 8	

■ Black Tolex covering; silver grille.
■ Black control panel (numbered); Six black knobs (Gain, t, m, frequency, b, master).
■ Speaker: 1 x 15in.
■ Solid state.
■ Output: 65W.
Made by Fender Japan.

SIDEKICK 65 REVERB

1986-1988	
CABINET: STYLE E	
NAMEPLATE: STYLE 8	

■ Black Tolex covering; silver grille.
■ Black control panel (numbered); 11 black knobs (Ch A: v, t, b. Ch B: v, gain, master, t, m, b, p, r).
■ Speaker: 1 x 12in.
■ Solid state.
■ Output: 65W.
Made by Fender Japan.

SIDEKICK 100 BASS

1986-1993	
CABINET: STYLE F	
NAMEPLATE: STYLE 8	

■ Black Tolex covering; silver grille.
■ Black control panel (numbered); Five black knobs (v, master, t, m, b).
■ Speaker: 1 x 15in Eminence in separate enclosure.
■ Solid state.
■ Output: 100W.
Also known as Fender 100 Bass Head.
Made by Fender Japan.

SK15B (or Squier SK15B)

1991-1994	
CABINET: STYLE E	
NAMEPLATE: STYLE 8	

■ Black Tolex covering; grey grille.
■ Black control panel (numbered); Four red knobs (v, t, m, b).
■ Speaker: 1 x 8in.
■ Solid state.
■ Output: 15W.
Budget bass amp. Soon to be replaced by BXR15.

SK CHORUS 20

INTRODUCED 1991	
CABINET: STYLE E	
NAMEPLATE: STYLE 8	

■ Black Tolex covering; black grille.
■ Black control panel (numbered); Ten red knobs (Overdrive, gain, v, t, m, b, p, chorus rate & depth).
■ Speakers: 2 x 8in.
■ Solid state.
■ Output: 2 x 10W.
Known as the Studio Lead 22SC in Japan, where it was made.
The Japanese version claims only 2 x 7W output.

SOLID STATE BASSMAN

1968-1970	
CABINET: STYLE H	
NAMEPLATE: see note	

■ Black Tolex covering; silver grille.
■ Aluminium control panel (nunbered); Four aluminium knobs (v, t, b, style).
■ Speakers: 3 x 12in.
■ Solid state.
■ Output: 100W.
Later renamed Transistor Bassman. Some have underlined Fender nameplate on grille.
Fender name appears in block letters painted on panel across grille.

SOLID STATE DELUXE REVERB

1967/8-1970	
CABINET: STYLE G	
NAMEPLATE: see note	

■ Black Tolex covering; silver grille.
■ Aluminium control panel (numbered); Nine aluminium knobs (Normal: bs, v, t, b. Vibrato, bs, v, t, b, r, s, i).
■ Speaker: 1 x 12in.
■ Solid state.
■ Output: 25W.
1969 models claim 32W output.
Part of Fender's most disastrous range. Fender name appears in block letters on aluminium panel across grille.

SOLID STATE PRO REVERB

1967/8-1970	
CABINET: STYLE G	
NAMEPLATE: see note	

■ Black Tolex covering; silver grille.
■ Aluminium control panel (numbered); Ten aluminium knobs (Normal: bs, v, t, b. Vibrato: bs, style, v, t, b, s, i, r).
■ Speakers: 2 x 12in.
■ Solid state.
■ Output: 50W.
Includes reverb footswitch. Fender name appears in block letters on panel across grille.

SOLID STATE SUPER REVERB

1967/8-1970	
CABINET: STYLE G	
NAMEPLATE: see note	

■ Black Tolex covering; silver grille.
■ Aluminium control panel (numbered); Nine aluminium knobs (Normal: bs, v, t, b. Vibrato: bs, v, t, b, r, s, i).
■ Speakers: 4 x 10in.
■ Solid state.
■ Output: 50W.
Fender name appears in block letters on panel across grille.

SOLID STATE VIBROLUX REVERB

1967/8-1970	
CABINET: STYLE G	
NAMEPLATE: see note	

■ Black Tolex covering; silver grille.
■ Aluminium control panel (numbered); Seven aluminium knobs (Normal: bs, v, t, b. Vibrato: bs, v, t, s, i).
■ Speakers: 2 x 10in.
■ Solid state.
■ Output: 35W.
Fender name appears in block letters on panel across grille.

SQUIER SKX15

1990-1993	
CABINET: STYLE E	
NAMEPLATE: STYLE 8	

■ Black Tolex covering; grey grille.
■ Black control panel (numbered); Five red knobs (Gain, v, t, b, contour) plus power shift switch.
■ Speaker: 1 x 8in.
■ Solid state.
■ Output: 15W.
Also packaged as Fender X-15. With reverb: SKX15R.
Part of Fender Japan's SKX range.

SQUIER SKX25R

1990-1993	
CABINET: STYLE E	
NAMEPLATE: STYLE 8	

■ Black Tolex covering; grey grille.
■ Black control panel (numbered); Five red knobs (Gain, v, t, b, contour) plus power shift switch.
■ Speaker: 1 x 10in.
■ Solid state.
■ Output: 25W.
Part of Fender Japan's SKX range.

SQUIER SKX35R

1990-1993	
CABINET: STYLE E	
NAMEPLATE: STYLE 8	

■ Black Tolex covering; grey grille.
■ Black control panel (numbered); Five red knobs (Gain, v, t, b, contour) plus power shift switch.
■ Speaker: 1 x 12in.
■ Solid state.
■ Output: 35W.
Part of Fender Japan's SKX range.

SQUIER SKX65R

1992-1993	
CABINET: STYLE E	
NAMEPLATE: STYLE 8	

■ Black Tolex covering; grey grille.
■ Black control panel (numbered); Eight red knobs (Ch A: v, t, b. Ch B: gain, v, t, b, contour) plus power shift switch.
■ Speaker: 1 x 12in.
■ Solid state.
■ Output: 65W.
Part of Fender Japan's SKX range.

SQUIER SKX100R

1992-1993	
CABINET: STYLE E	
NAMEPLATE: STYLE 8	

■ Black Tolex covering; grey grille.
■ Black control panel (numbered); Eight red knobs (Ch A: v, b, t. Ch B: gain, v, t, b, contour) plus power shift switch.
■ Speakers: 2 x 12in.
■ Solid state.
■ Output: 100W.
Part of Fender Japan's SKX range.

SQUIER 15

INTRODUCED 1988	
CABINET: STYLE E	
NAMEPLATE: STYLE 8	

■ Black Tolex covering; black grille.
■ Black control panel (numbered); Six black knobs (v, gain, master, t, m, b).
■ Speaker: 1 x 8in.
■ Solid state.
■ Output: 15W.
Also known as Sidekick 15.
Current version is made in Mexico.

STAGE LEAD CBS

1983-1985	
CABINET: STYLE E	
NAMEPLATE: STYLE 9	

■ Black Tolex covering; silver grille.
■ New blackface control panel; 11 silver-top numbered knobs (Ch 1: V, t, m, b. Ch 2: v, gain, master, t, m, b, r).
■ Speaker: 1 x 12in.
■ Solid state.
■ Output: 100W.
Channel switching solid state amp. High power version of Studio Lead.

STAGE LEAD 212 CBS

1983-1985	
CABINET: STYLE E	
NAMEPLATE: STYLE 9	

■ Black Tolex covering; silver grille.
■ New blackface control panel; 11 silver-top numbered knobs (Ch 1: V, t, m, b. Ch 2: v, gain, master, t, m, b, r).
■ Speakers: 2 x 12in.
■ Solid state.
■ Output: 100W.
Channel switching solid state amp. Twin speaker version of Stage Lead.

STAGE 112SE Post-CBS

INTRODUCED 1992	
CABINET: STYLE E	
NAMEPLATE: STYLE 9	

■ Black Tolex covering; silver grille.
■ Black control panel (numbered); Ten black knobs (Normal: v, t, m, b. Drive: gain, contour, t, b, v, r).
■ Speaker: 1 x 12in.
■ Solid state.
■ Output: 160W.
Derived from original Fast Four. Single speaker version of Pro 185.

STAGE 185 Post-CBS

1989-1992	
CABINET: STYLE E	
NAMEPLATE: STYLE 9	

■ Black Tolex covering; black grille.
■ Black control panel (numbered); 12 red knobs (Ch 1: v, t, b. Ch 2: gain, boost, t, m, b, contour, p, r, v).
■ Speakers: 1 x 12in Eminence.
■ Solid state.
■ Output: 160W.
Single speaker version of Pro 185.

STUDENT
See Champion, Champ and Princeton

There is a great confusion between the Student, Princeton and Champion amps. Packaged for music students.

STUDIO BASS

1977-1982	
CABINET: STYLE E	
NAMEPLATE: STYLE 8	

■ Black Tolex covering; black grille with white surround.
■ New blackface control panel; Twelve silver-top numbered knobs (v, t, m, b, p, distortion, output level and five-way equalisation).
■ Speaker: 1 x 15in Electrovoice.
■ Valves: 2 x 7025, 12AT7, 12AU7A, 12AX7A, 6 x 6L6.
■ Output: 200W.
Remodelled in 1981.
Bass version of Super Twin.

STUDIO LEAD

1983-1985	
CABINET: STYLE E	
NAMEPLATE: STYLE 9	

■ Black Tolex covering; silver grille.
■ New blackface control panel; 11 silver-top numbered knobs (Ch 1: V, t, m, b. Ch 2: v, gain, master, t, m, b, r).
■ Speaker: 1 x 12in.
■ Solid state.
■ Output: 50W.
Channel switching solid state amp. Low power version of Stage Lead.

STUDIO 85
1988
CABINET: STYLE E
NAMEPLATE: STYLE 9

■ Black Tolex covering; black grille.
■ Black control panel (numbered); Nine red knobs (v, t, m, b, r, gain, limiter, p, v).
■ Speakers: 1 x 12in Eminence.
■ Solid state.
■ Output: 65W.
Immediately renamed 85 on introduction.

SUPER V-front
1947-1952
CABINET: V-front
NAMEPLATE: STYLE 1

■ Early tweed covering; dark brown grille with chrome strip.
■ Top control panel (numbered); Three pointer knobs (Mic v, inst v, tone).
■ Speakers: 2 x 10in Jensen.
■ Valves: 5U4, 2 x 6L6, 3 x 6SC7.
■ Output: 16W.
Changes to 12AX7 and 12AY7 miniature type valves as soon as they become available. NB, there is no TV front Super. Loses V-front and becomes wide panel from 1952. Some Supers have 6V6 valves. Renamed version of Dual Professional.

SUPER Wide panel
1952-1954
CABINET: STYLE C
NAMEPLATE: STYLE 1

■ Diagonal tweed covering; brown cloth grille.
■ Top control panel (numbered); Three pointer knobs (Mic v, inst v, tone).
■ Speakers: 2 x 10in Jensen.
■ Valves: 2 x 12AY7, 12AX7, 2 x 6L6G, 5U4G.
■ Output: 20W.
Some Supers have 6V6 valves.
Distinctive V-front and chrome strip removed from 1952.

SUPER Narrow panel
1954-1960
CABINET: STYLE D
NAMEPLATE: STYLE 2

■ Diagonal tweed covering; brown tweed-era grille.
■ Top control panel (numbered); Four pointer knobs (Mic v, inst v, b, t).
■ Speakers: 2 x 10in Jensen.
■ Valves: 2 x 12AY7, 12AX7, 2 x 6L6G, 5U4G.
■ Output: 20W.
Some narrow panel Supers have 6V6s. Nameplate changes to script type in 1955. Then Fender Super Amp, script, from 1956. Presence control added 1958.
Note separate tone controls.

SUPER Brownface
1960-1964
CABINET: STYLE E
NAMEPLATE: STYLE 6

■ Brown Tolex covering; brown tweed-era grille.
■ Brownface control panel (numbered); Nine brown knobs (Normal: v, b, t. Vibrato, v, b, t, s, i. Both: p).
■ Speakers: 2 x 10in Jensen.
■ Valves: 5 x 7025, 2 x 6L6GC, 5U4G.
■ Output: 30W.
From about 1962 some have 5881 output section and are capable of 45W. Replaced by Super/Reverb.

SUPER 60
1989-1993
CABINET: STYLE E
NAMEPLATE: STYLE 9

■ Black Tolex covering; black grille.
■ Black control panel (numbered); Eight red knobs (Ch A: v, t, m, b; Ch B: v, gain. Both: p, r).
■ Speakers: 1 x 12in Eminence.
■ Valves: 2 x 12AX7, 12AT7, 2 x 6L6.
■ Output: 60W.
The red knobs were soon replaced by black ones.
Top and rack mounted versions also exist.

SUPER 112
1988-1993
CABINET: STYLE E
NAMEPLATE: STYLE 9

■ Black Tolex covering; black grille.
■ Black control panel (numbered); Eight red knobs (Ch A: clean, bs. Ch B: overdrive v, gain. Both: t, m, b, r, p) plus notch filter.
■ Speakers: 1 x 12in Eminence.
■ Valves: 2 x 12AX7, 12AT7, 2 x 6L6.
■ Output: 60W.
The red knobs were soon replaced by black ones. Celestion speakers were an option.

SUPER 210
1988-1993
CABINET: STYLE E
NAMEPLATE: STYLE 9

■ Black Tolex covering; black grille.
■ Black control panel (numbered); Eight red knobs (Ch A: clean, bs; Ch B: overdrive v, gain. Both t, m, b, r, p) plus notch filter.
■ Speakers: 2 x 10in Eminence.
■ Valves: 2 x 12AX7, 12AT7, 2 x 6L6.
■ Output: 60W.
The red knobs were soon replaced by black ones.
Identical to Super 112 except speakers.

SUPER AMP Post-CBS
INTRODUCED 1992
CABINET: STYLE E
NAMEPLATE: STYLE 7

■ Black Tolex covering; silver grille.
■ New blackface control panel; 12 silver-top numbered knobs (Ch 1: v, t, b, m. Ch 2: gain 1, gain 2, t, b, m, v. Mix and r for both channels).
■ Speakers: 4 x 10in with AlNiCo magnets.
■ Valves: 4 x 12AX7, 2 x 12AT7, 2 x 6L6.
■ Output: 60W.
Part of current Pro Tube series. Derived from 1988 Super 112/210.

SUPER BASSMAN
1970-1972
CABINET: STYLE F
NAMEPLATE: STYLE 7

■ Black Tolex covering; silver grille.
■ Silverface control panel; Seven silver-top numbered knobs (Bass: ds, v, t, b. Normal: bs, v, t, m, b).
■ Speakers: 2 x 15in.
■ Valves: 2 x 7025, 12AT7, 4 x 6L6GC, silicon rectifiers.
■ Output: 100W.
If used with two speaker cabinets this is known as the Super Bassman II. Later renamed Bassman 100.

SUPER CHAMP
1982-1985
CABINET: STYLE E
NAMEPLATE: STYLE 9

■ Black Tolex covering; silver grille.
■ New blackface control panel; Six silver-top numbered knobs (v, t, b, r, lead level, master v).
■ Speaker: 1 x 10in.
■ Valves: 2 x 7025, 2 x 6V6GTA, silicon rectifiers.

■ Output: 18W.
Also available with Electro-voice speaker as an option. The Champ II is a budget version.
Incorporates reverb and switchable lead sound using the reverb drive as an extra pre-amp stage.

SUPER REVERB *Blackface/Silverface*

	1964-1982
CABINET:	STYLE E
NAMEPLATE:	STYLE 7

■ Black Tolex covering; silver grille.
■ Blackface control panel; 11 silver-top numbered knobs (Normal: bs, v, t, m, b. Vibrato: v, t, m, b, r, s, i).
■ Speakers: 4 x 10in.
■ Valves: 3 x 7025, 12AX7, 2 x 12AT7, 2 x 6L6GC.
■ Output: 40W.
Silverface from 1968 has various unhelpful modifications to the output stage. Power increased to 45W from 1970. Master volume and distortion switch from 1976. Power raised to 70W for new blackface model of 1981.

SUPER REVERB SOLID STATE
See SOLID STATE

SUPER SHOWMAN

	1970-1972
CABINET:	STYLE F
NAMEPLATE:	see note

■ Black Tolex covering.
■ Black/aluminium control panel; 18 aluminium numbered knobs (Including Normal: bs, v, t, b. Sound expander: v, t, b, fuzz, dimension IV. Vibrato/reverb: s, i, r, master v).
■ Speakers: 4 x 12in or 8 x 10in.
■ Solid state (49 transistors and 19 diodes).
■ Output: 140W.
A total departure: a three channel pre-amp coupled with powered speakers. Designed by Seth Lover. Fender name appears on aluminium panel at top of grille.

SUPER SIX REVERB

	1970-1979
CABINET:	STYLE E
NAMEPLATE:	STYLE 7

■ Black Tolex covering; silver grille.
■ Silverface control panel; 12 silver-top numbered knobs (Normal: bs, v, t, m, b. Vibrato: bs, v, t, m, b, r, s, i. master v).
■ Valves: 3 x 7025, 2 x 12AT7, 12AX7A, 4 x 6L6GC.
■ Output: 100W.
1976 has distortion switch on master volume control.
The Twin Reverb in a different guise.

SUPER TWIN

	1976-1981
CABINET:	STYLE E
NAMEPLATE:	STYLE 8

■ Black Tolex covering; black grill with white surround.
■ New blackface control panel; 12 silver-top numbered knobs (v, t, m, b, p, distortion, output level and five-way equalisation).
■ Speakers: 2 x 12in.
■ Valves: 2 x 7025, 12AT7, 12AU7A, 12AX7A, 6 x 6L6.
■ Output: 180W.
Remodelled in more traditional look in 1981 before being dropped.

TAURUS

	1970-1972
CABINET:	STYLE E
NAMEPLATE:	STYLE 7

■ Black Tolex covering; silver grille.
■ Black/aluminium control panel; 10 numbered aluminium knobs

(Normal: bs, v, t, b. Vibrato: bs, v, t, m, b, r, s, i).
■ Speakers: 2 x 10in JBL.
■ Solid state.
■ Output: 42W.

THE TWIN *Post-CBS*

INTRODUCED	1987
CABINET:	STYLE E
NAMEPLATE:	STYLE 9

■ Black Tolex covering; black grille.
■ Black control panel (numbered); 11 knobs (Ch 1: v, t, m, b. Ch 2: gain, t, m, b, p, v, r) plus numerous pull switches.
■ Speakers: 2 x 12in Eminence.
■ Valves: 2 x 12AT7, 5 x 12AX7, 4 x 6L6.
■ Output: 100W.
Available in white, grey, red or snakeskin on special order. Revised with black knobs and silver grille in 1992.
First new amp by the new Fender company which started in 1985.

TONE-MASTER *From the Custom Shop*

INTRODUCED	1993
CABINET:	STYLE F
NAMEPLATE:	STYLE 6

■ Cream Tolex covering; black grille.
■ Brownface control panel; Nine cream knobs (Ch 1: v, t, m, b. Ch 2: v, t, m, b, r).
■ 4 x 12in or 2 x 12in Celestion in separate cab.
■ Valves: 3 x 12AX7, 4 x 6L6.
■ Output: 100W.
From the Custom Shop.

TRANSISTOR BASSMAN

	1970-1972
CABINET:	STYLE H
NAMEPLATE:	see note

■ Black Tolex covering; silver grille.
■ Aluminium control panel (numbered); Four aluminium knobs (v, t, b, style).
■ Speakers: 3 x 12in cabinet.
■ Solid state.
■ Output: 105W.
The amp is virtually identical to the Solid State Bassman, with slightly different cosmetics.
The sole survivor of the previous generation of solid state equipment. Fender name appears on amp panel and on aluminium panel across grille.

TREMOLUX *Narrow panel*

	1955-1960
CABINET:	STYLE D
NAMEPLATE:	STYLE 2

■ Diagonal tweed covering; brown tweed-era grille.
■ Top control panel (numbered); Five pointer knobs (Mic v, Inst v, tone, s, depth).
■ Speaker: 1 x 12in.
■ Valves: 12AY7, 2 x 12AX7, 2 x 6V6.
■ Output: 15W.
Later tweed models have different phase inverter and tremolo circuits. Nameplate 3 after about 1957.
First Fender amp with electronic tremolo.

TREMOLUX *Piggy-back*

	1961-1966
CABINET:	STYLE F
NAMEPLATE:	STYLE 6

■ Cream Tolex covering; maroon grille.
■ Brownface control panel (numbered); Eight cream knobs (Bright: v, t, b. Normal: v, t, b. Both: s, i).
■ Speaker: 1 x 10in cabinet.
■ Valves: 2 x 7025, 2 x 12AX7, 2 x 6L6GC.
■ Output: 30W.

Cabinet has 2 x 10in speakers from 1962. Blackface look and bright switches from 1964. Pre-amp valves change to 12AX7 and 12AT7 from 1964.
Basically the same chassis as the Vibrolux, Concert, Pro and Bandmaster of the same vintage: different power amp voltages give different outputs.

TWIN AMP *Wide panel*

1952-1954
CABINET: STYLE C
NAMEPLATE: STYLE 1

- Diagonal tweed covering; brown cloth grille.
- Top control panel (numbered); Four pointer knobs (mic v, inst v, b, t).
- Speakers: 2 x 12in Jensen.
- Valves: 2 x 6SC7. Tone controls: 6J5. Driver: 6SC7. 2x6L6.
- Output: 15W.

The first amp in wide-panel style.

TWIN AMP *Narrow panel*

1954-1960
CABINET: STYLE D
NAMEPLATE: STYLE 2

- Diagonal tweed covering; brown tweed-era grille.
- Top control panel (numbered); Five pointer knobs (mic v, inst v, b, t, p).
- Speakers: 2 x 12in Jensen.
- Valves: 3 x 12AY7, 12AX7, 2 x 6L6, 2 x 5Y3GY.
- Output: 50W.

Collectors say that some early narrow panel Twins have 2 x 10in speakers. Mid range control and bright and normal inputs from 1956. Changes to 2 x 5U4GA, then GZ34. From 1958, pre-amp/driver valves change to one 12AY7 and 2 x 12AX7. Four 5881 output valves are used to give about 85W output.
The flagship combo in the Fender range.

TWIN AMP *Brownface*

1960-1963
CABINET: STYLE E
NAMEPLATE: STYLE 6

- Cream Tolex covering; maroon or light brown grille.
- Brownface control panel (numbered); Nine cream knobs (Normal: v, t, b. Vibrato: v, t, b, s, i. Both: p).
- Speakers: 2 x 12in Jensen.
- Valves: 4 x 7025, 2 x 12AX7, 4 x 6L6GC. Rectifiers: solid state.
- Output: 90W.

Model 6G8A, the final variant, uses 6 x 7025 and 4 x 5881 valves.
Replaced by Twin Reverb.

TWIN REVERB *Blackface/silverface*

1963/4-1982
CABINET: STYLE E
NAMEPLATE: STYLE 7

- Black Tolex covering; silver grille.
- Blackface control panel; 11 silver-top numbered knobs (Normal: bs, v, t, m, b. Vibrato: bs, v, t, m, b, r, s, i).
- Speakers: 2 x 12in Jensen.
- Valves: 3 x 7025, 2 x 12AT7, 12AX7, 4 x 6L6GC.
- Output: 85W.

Silverface version is virtually identical. 1973 model boasts 100W and includes a master volume control. 1976 adds pull distortion switch to master volume. JBLs available as an option 1981 model is blackface again and has 135W output: it uses 4 x 7025, 2 x 12AX7 and 4 6L6GCs.
The classic Fender amp. Variants of this chassis were used in many other amps, including the Vibrosonic Reverb, Showman Reverb, Super Six Reverb and Quad Reverb.

'65 TWIN REVERB *Vintage reissue*

INTRODUCED 1992
CABINET: STYLE E
NAMEPLATE: STYLE 7

Black Tolex covering; silver grille.

- Blackface control panel; 11 silver-top numbered knobs (Normal: bs, v, t, m, b. Vibrato: bs, v, , m, b, r, s, i).
- Speakers: 2 x 12in.
- Valves: 4 x 12AX7, 2, x 12AT7, 4 x 6L6GC.
- Output: 85W.

Recreation of pre-CBS Twin Reverb.

TWIN REVERB II

1983-1985
CABINET: STYLE E
NAMEPLATE: STYLE 8

- Black Tolex covering; silver grille.
- New blackface control panel; 12 silver-top numbered knobs (Ch 1: v, t, m, b. Ch 2: v, gain, master, t, m, b, r, p).
- Speakers: 2 x 12in.
- Valves: 4 x 7025, 2 x 12AT7, 2 x 6L6GC.
- Output: 105W.

Also produced in a Top/head version.
Adds channel switching and an effects loop to the classical form of the Twin Reverb.

ULTRA CHORUS

INTRODUCED 1993
CABINET: STYLE E
NAMEPLATE: STYLE 9

- Black Tolex covering; silver grille.
- Black control panel (numbered); 14 black knobs (Normal: v, t, m, b, r. Drive: gain, contour, v, t, m, b, r, chorus rate & depth).
- Speakers: 2 x 12in.
- Solid state.
- Output: 2 x 65W.

Derived from Power Chorus.

VIBRASONIC *Brownface*

1959-1963
CABINET: STYLE E
NAMEPLATE: STYLE 6

- Brown Tolex covering; brown tweed-era grille.
- Brownface control panel; Nine brown knobs (Normal: b, t, v. Vibrato: b, t, v, s, i. Both: p).
- Speaker: 1 x 15in JBL.
- Valves: 5 x 7025, 2 x 6L6GC.
- Output: 25W.

Odd reverse control layout soon abandoned. Some may be in cream Tolex. Later versions use 2 x 12AX7s in the tremolo circuit instead of one of the 7025s, and 5881s in the output stage.
Essentially a Pro amp with a 15in JBL speaker and vibrato.

VIBRASONIC REVERB *Silverface*

1972-1979
CABINET: STYLE E
NAMEPLATE: STYLE 7

- Black Tolex covering; silver grille.
- Silverface control panel; 12 silver-top numbered knobs (Normal: bs, v, t, m, b. Vibrato: bs, v, t, m, b, r, s, i. Both: master v).
- Speaker: 1 x 15in.
- Valves: 3 x 7025, 2 x 12AT7, 12AX7, 4 x 6L6GC.
- Output: 100W.

1976: distortion switch added to master volume.
A Silverface Twin Reverb with a 15in speaker. Nothing much to do with earlier Vibrasonic.

VIBRO CHAMP *Blackface/silverface*

1964-1979
CABINET: STYLE E
NAMEPLATE: NONE

- Black Tolex covering; silver grille.
- Blackface control panel; Five silver-top numbered knobs (v, t, b, s, i).
- Speaker: 1 x 8in.
- Valves: 2 x 12AX7A, 6V6GY, 5Y3GT.

■ Output: 4W.
1969: silverface, 5W output. 1972, 6W output. Some have nameplates from about 1966.
Champ with a tremolo circuit.

VIBRO-KING *From the Custom Shop*

INTRODUCED 1993	
CABINET: STYLE E	
NAMEPLATE: STYLE 6	

■ Cream Tolex covering; black grille.
■ Black control panel (numbered); Nine cream knobs (Ch 1: v, t, b. Ch 2: v, t, m, b. Both: s, i).
■ Speakers: 3 x 10in with AlNiCo magnets.
■ Valves: 5 x 12AX7, 2 x 6L6, EL84.
■ Output: 60W.
First product of Fender's custom shop.

VIBROLUX *Narrow panel*

1956-1961	
CABINET: STYLE D	
NAMEPLATE: STYLE 2	

■ Diagonal tweed covering; brown tweed-era grille.
■ Top control panel (numbered); Four pointer knobs (v, tone, s, depth).
■ Speaker: 1 x 10in Jensen.
■ Valves: 2 x 12AX7, 2 x 6V6.
■ Output: 10W.
Nameplates 3 and 5 appear later.
Using half the first pre-amp valve for tremolo duties cuts output power.

VIBROLUX *Brownface/Blackface*

1961-1965	
CABINET: STYLE E	
NAMEPLATE: NONE	

■ Brown Tolex covering; light brown grille.
■ Brownface control panel; Eight brown knobs (Normal: v, b, t. Bright: v, b, t. Both: s, i).
■ Speakers: 1 x 12in Jensen.
■ Valves: 2 x 7025, 2 x 12AX7, 2 x 6L6GC.
■ Output: 30W.
Blackface from 1964 puts speed and intensity controls on vibrato channel only and gives both channels bright switches. One 12AX7 becomes a 12AT7. Nameplate 7 from about 1966.
The amp is identical to the Tremolux of the same era.

VIBROLUX REVERB *Blackface/silverface*

1964-1979	
CABINET: STYLE E	
NAMEPLATE: NONE	

■ Black Tolex covering; silver grille.
■ Blackface control panel; Nine silver-top numbered knobs (Normal: bs, v, t, b. Vibrato: bs, v, t, b, r, s, i).
■ Speakers: 2 x 10in.
■ Valves: 3 x 7025, 2 x 12AT7, 12AX7, 2 x 6L6GC.
■ Output: 35W.
Silver grille face version has 40W output from 1970. Nameplate 7 from about 1966, nameplate 8 from 1976.
Sometimes called the poor man's Twin, despite having 10in speakers and much lower output.

VIBROLUX REVERB SOLID STATE
See SOLID SXTATE

VIBROVERB *Brownface*

1963-1964	
CABINET: STYLE E	
NAMEPLATE: STYLE 6	

■ Brown Tolex covering; light brown grille.
■ Brownface control panel (numbered); Nine brown knobs (Normal: v, t, b. Bright: v, t, b, r. Speed and intensity for both channels.)
■ Speakers: 2 x 10in.

■ Valves: 4 x 7025, 2 x 12AX7, 2 x 6L6GC, GZ34.
■ Output: 35W.

VIBROVERB *Blackface*

1964-1965	
CABINET: STYLE E	
NAMEPLATE: STYLE 7	

■ Black Tolex covering; silver grille.
■ Blackface control panel; Nine silver-top numbered knobs (Normal: bs, v, t, b. Vibrato: bs, v, t, b, r, s, i).
■ Speaker: 1 x 15in.
■ Valves: 3 x 7025, 12AX7, 2 x 12AT7, 2 x 6L6GC, GZ34.
■ Output: 40W.
Second version of Vibroverb has different tremolo and phase inverter circuitry. Effectively replaced by Vibrolux Reverb.

WHITE

1955	
NARROW PANEL	
NAMEPLATE: WHITE	

■ Grey fabric covering; blue-black grille.
■ Top control panel (numbered); Two pointer knobs (v, tone).
■ Speaker: 1 x 8in.
■ Valves: 12AX7, 6V6, 5Y3.
■ Output: 3W.
A student amp (with a matching steel guitar) produced by Leo Fender in 1955 as a brief tribute to Forrest White.

X-15

1991-1992	
CABINET: STYLE E	
NAMEPLATE: STYLE 8	

■ Black Tolex covering; black grille.
■ Black control panel (numbered); Five red knobs (Gain, v, t, b, contour) plus power shift switch.
■ Speaker: 1 x 8in.
■ Solid state.
■ Output: 15W.
Also packaged as Squier SKX15 and SKX15R (with reverb).
From Fender Japan.

YALE REVERB

1982-1985	
CABINET: STYLE E	
NAMEPLATE: STYLE 9	

■ Black Tolex covering; silver grille.
■ New blackface control panel; Seven silver-top numbered knobs (v, gain, master, t, m, b, r).
■ Speaker: 1 x 12in.
■ Solid state.
■ Output: 50W.
Effectively the Harvard Reverb II with a 12in speaker.

'63 VIBROVERB *Vintage reissue*

INTRODUCED 1990	
CABINET: STYLE E	
NAMEPLATE: STYLE 6	

■ Brown Tolex covering; light brown grille.
■ Brownface control panel (numbered); Nine brown knobs (Normal: v, t, b. Bright: v, t, b, r. Both: s, i).
■ Speakers: 2 x 10in.
■ Valves: 4 x 12AX7, 2 x 12AT7, 2 x 6L6GC, GZ34.
■ Output: 40W.
Meticulously created reproduction of extremely rare amplifier. Part of Vintage series.

30

1979-1982	
CABINET: STYLE E	
NAMEPLATE: STYLE 9	

■ Black Tolex covering; silver grille.
■ New blackface control panel; Nine silver-top numbered knobs (normal: v, t, b. Reverb: gain, t, m, b, r, v).
■ Speakers: 2 x 10in or 1 x 12in.
■ Valves: 3 x 7025, 2 x 12AT7, 2 x 6L6GC.
■ Output: 30W.

75
1979-1983
CABINET: STYLE E
NAMEPLATE: STYLE 9

■ Black Tolex covering; silver grille.
■ New blackface control panel; Eight silver-top numbered knobs (Ch 1: gain, t, m, b. Ch 2: lead drive, r, lead level, master v).
■ Speaker: 1 x 15in.
■ Valves: 3 x 7025, 2 x 12AT7, 2 x 6L6GC.
■ Output: 75W.
Also available as head amp version.

85
1988-1992
CABINET: STYLE E
NAMEPLATE: STYLE 9

■ Black Tolex covering; black grille.
■ Black control panel (numbered); Nine red knobs (V, t, m, b, r, gain, limiter, p, v).
■ Speaker: 1 x 12in Eminence.
■ Solid state.
■ Output: 65W.
The current Fender regime's first attempt at solid state.
Now discontinued.

140
1979-1982
CABINET: STYLE H
NAMEPLATE: STYLE 9

■ Black Tolex covering.
■ New blackface control panel; Eight silver-top numbered knobs (v, t, m, b, r, 5 band graphic eq, lead drive, lead level, master v).
■ Head amp only.
■ Valves: 4 x 7025, 2 x 12AT7, 4 x 6L6GC.
■ Output: 135W.

300PS
1976-1979
CABINET: STYLE H
NAMEPLATE: STYLE 8

■ Black Tolex covering; black foam grille.
■ Black control panel; 12 silver-top numbered knobs (v, t, m, b, p, 5-way eq, distortion, output).
■ Speakers: 4 x 12in.
■ Valves: 2 x 7025, 12AT7, 6V6, 4 x 6550.
■ Output: 300W.
Also available as 300PS Bass, with larger speaker cabinet.
Lower power variant of 400PS remarketed as a guitar amp.

400PS BASS
1970-1975
CABINET: STYLE H
NAMEPLATE: STYLE 7

■ Black Tolex covering; black foam grille.
■ Black control panel; 11 numbered knobs (Bass: ds, v, t, b. Normal: s, v, t, m, b, r, s, i, maste v).
■ Speaker: 18in in horn cabinet.
■ Valves: 6 x 7025, 12AT7, 6 x 6550.
■ Output: 435W.
most un-Fenderlike venture into heavy-duty bass amplification. Three mplifiers producing 145W each into a massive folded horn cabinet.

OWNERS' CREDITS
Amplifiers photographed came from the following individuals' and organisations' collections, and we are most grateful for their help. (The owners are listed here in the alphabetical order of the code used to identify their amps in the Key To Amp Photographs below.)
AH Alan Hardtke; **AR** Alan Rogan; **CM** Chuck Mason; **FE** Fender A&R; **JM** John Morrish; **MG** Music Ground.

KEY TO AMP PHOTOGRAPHS
The following key is designed to identify who owned which amps when they were photographed for the book. After the relevant page number we list the model followed by its owner's initials in bold letters (check the Owners' Credits above). For example '6-7: K&F **AH**' means that the K&F amp shown across pages 6 and 7 was owned by Alan Hardtke.

Jacket front: Bandmaster **AR**. *6-7:* K&F **AH**. *8:* Deluxe Model 26 **AH**. *9:* Super **AH**. *12:* Champion 600 **AH**. *13:* Champion 800 **AH**. *15:* Deluxe **AR**. *22:* Bassman **AR**. *23:* Tremolux **AH**. *24:* Vibrasonic **AR**. *25:* Showman **AR**. *26:* Reverbs **AR**. *27:* Twin Reverb **AR**. *36:* Twin Reverb **MG**; Dual Showman Reverb **MG**; Bassman **MG**. *40:* Super Six Reverb **CM**. *44-45:* Concert 112 **MG**. *49:* London Reverb **MG**. *52:* Squier 15 **FE**; Switcher **JM**. *56:* Pro 185 **MG**. *57:* Princeton Chorus **MG**. *59:* M-80 **FE**; J.A.M. **MG**. *60:* ´63 Vibroverb **FE**; ´65 Twin Reverb **FE**. *61:* ´65 Deluxe Reverb **FE**; ´59 Bassman **FE**. *64:* Performer 1000 **FE**. *65:* Blues De Ville **FE**. *66:* Vibro-King **FE**; Tone-Master **FE**. *Jacket back:* Bassman **AR**.

All amplifier photography is by Nigel Bradley, of Visuel 7.

MEMORABILIA including catalogues, brochures, magazines and photographs comes from the collections of Tony Bacon and of Paul Day. Each item was photographed in strict scientific conditions by Nigel Bradley and Will Taylor of Visuel 7, London.

INTERVIEWS
Unsourced quotations in the text are from interviews conducted by John Morrish during 1994.

IN ADDITION to those named above in Owners' Credits, JOHN MORRISH would like to thank: Tony Bacon (Balafon); Gary Bohannon; Bill Carson (Fender); Walter Carter; Patrick Chelling (Orange County Register); Pete Cornish; Paul Day; George Fullerton; Rick Harrison (Music Ground); Bill Hughes (Fender); Sam Hutton; Ed Jahns; Mike Lewis (Fender); Jon Lewin (Making Music); Tom Nolan (Fender); John Peden; Don Randall; Bob Rissi; Paul Rivera; Deborah Thorp; Norma Velvikis (Phelps); Forrest White; Ian Woodall (Arbiter). BALAFON would like to thank: Walter Carter; Paul Day; Justin Harrison, Steve Fidler and Graham Sutherland (Music Ground); Chris Mason; Tom Nolan (Fender); Steve Park (Live Music); John Peden.

BIBLIOGRAPHY
Tony Bacon & Paul Day *The Fender Book* (IMP/Miller Freeman 1992); Donald Brosnac *The Amp Book* (Paul C's Guitar Products 1983); Bureau of Naval Personnel *Basic Electronics* (Dover 1973); Ritchie Flieger *Amps! The Other Half of Rock'n'Roll* (Hal Leonard 1993); *The Amplifier* (Rittor 1993); George Fullerton *Guitar Legends* (Centerstream 1993); Aspen Pittman *The Tube Amp Book* 4th edition (Groove Tubes 1993); M G Scroggie *Foundations of Wireless* (Iliffe 1958); Van Valkenburgh, Nooger & Neville Inc *Basic Electronics* (Technical Press 1964); Gerald Weber *A Desktop Reference of Hip Vintage Guitar Amps* (Kendrick 1994); Forrest White *Fender The Inside Story* (Miller Freeman 1994).